Prayers That Avail Much®
for Grandparents
James 5:16

by
Germaine Copeland
Word Ministries, Inc.

And this is the confidence that we have in him, that, if we ask any thing according to his will, he heareth us: and if we know that he hear us, whatsoever we ask, we know that we have the petitions that we desired of him.

1 John 5:14,15

Harrison House
Tulsa, Oklahoma

10 09 08 07 06 05   10 9 8 7 6 5 4 3 2 1

Prayers That Avail Much® for Grandparents
ISBN 1-57794-723-1
Copyright © 2005 by Germaine Copeland
38 Sloan Street
Roswell, Georgia 30075

Published by Harrison House, Inc.
P.O. Box 35035
Tulsa, Oklahoma 74153

CONTENTS

Part 3: Personal Prayers

Introduction

Then we Your people, the sheep of Your pasture, will give You thanks forever; we will show forth and publish Your praise from generation to generation.

Psalm 79:13 AMP

Grandparents are a vital link between generations, and God wants to use you as an instrument of righteousness in the life of your grandchildren. Your prayers, encouragement, and unconditional love are vital to their future whether you live near or far away. Jesus gives the conditions for answered prayer in John 15:7-8 (RSV): "If you abide in me, and my words abide in you, ask whatever you will, and it shall be done for you. By this my Father is glorified, that you bear much fruit, and so prove to be my disciples." Praying the scriptural prayers in this book will establish God's Word in the midst of you. Your prayers for your grandchildren will bear much fruit, and your faith will live on in the hearts of your children and grandchildren. My grandmothers, Mrs. Lennie Elkins Brock and Mrs. Annie Kelley Griffin, left a legacy of prayer; their prayers produced much fruit to the glory of the Father.

I only saw my grandparents once, sometimes twice each year, but the stamina of my grandmothers and the outgoing nature of my Papa Brock helped shape me into the person I am today. (My Grandfather Griffin died when my dad was a teenager, so I never knew him.)

My grandmothers were women who manifested strength in very different circumstances. Mama Brock taught me to lighten up, to be sensitive to the feelings of others, and to stand strong in adverse situations. She cared for my grandfather after a stroke that left him paralyzed on one side of his body and unable to communicate. Mama Brock was a woman of prayer. Before his stroke, Papa would kneel with her while she prayed before each meal. She never failed to pray and care for her family. When she lost her eyesight, her only complaint was that she could no longer take care of her husband.

My Granny Griffin, who managed a farm and raised her younger children after the death of her husband, left us a legacy of prayer and faith in the God who always provides. Three times each day family and visitors would sit down at the table loaded with many dishes of yummy food, but no one ate until they slipped down beside their chairs to kneel while she prayed. There was no doubt that you had been prayed for when you arose to sit down at the table once again. I can't remember anyone ever complaining about this custom. She prayed for her family every day.

My parents, Rev. A. H. "Buck" and Donnis Griffin, left their grandchildren a legacy of faith in the God who heals. The first thirteen years of his life David, our son, had asthma. On many occasions we had to take him to the emergency room, where he received the help he needed to breathe. His grandparents were visiting us one day when David was struggling to get his breath. My dad said, "God will heal David of this asthma." He and my mother laid hands on him and prayed the prayer of faith; David was healed! This memory of God's blessing from one generation to another has never faded. My children share this with their children.

My husband and I have eleven grandchildren and several great-grandchildren. While we were visiting our daughter and her family who live in Florida, Griffin, our four-year-old grandson, was having a difficult evening. Nothing pleased him, and he refused to obey or be comforted. After all else failed, his dad picked him up and carted him off to bed. Soon Griffin was asleep. The next morning his grandfather and I drove Griffin to preschool. Knowing that his teacher read special notes from parents or grandparents to the children each day, I handed her a note that I had written. "Griffin, Granddaddy and I are so proud of you. You are learning to make wise choices! Love, Nonna." He referred to the note later in the day, telling me that he is going to make wise choices. It wasn't the first note that I had written to him.

Whether you have full responsibility for your grand-children or part-time-hands-on responsibility, engage them in activities that you enjoy, talk to them about your interests, and listen to the things that are important to them. Take time to laugh with them, go for walks with them, tuck them in bed, and pray with them.

The prayers in this book are written to build you up, to prepare you to be there in special ways for your grand-children, and to help you pray effectively for them. As you share your time and energy with your grandchildren, they will observe and learn from you about life. Share the more abundant life—the life that Jesus gives.

A Word to Grandparents

My dear fellow grandparents,

At the time of this writing my grandchildren range in age from a few months old to thirty years old. From the beginning it has been my heart's desire to help mold them into the men and women God planned for them to be. Grandchildren didn't come with an instruction book, and I've had to learn where my responsibility begins and ends. There are things I can't change, but I am confident of this very thing: that He who began a good work in them will perform it until the day of Christ Jesus. He is able to keep all my grandchildren, from the oldest to the youngest.

Whatever plans you may have for this season of your life, I encourage you to make room for your grandchildren: give them the benefit of your years of experience. My mother-in-law, Mrs. Evelyn Copeland, says it takes a lifetime to learn how to live. While these children are in their formative years, share not just token gifts (which they love); share yourself with them. Talk with them, laugh with them, and cry with them. Become a safe place for them to pour out their thoughts and feelings. Your grandchildren will learn from observing you, just as I learned from mine.

God knows the beginning from the end, and we are somewhere in between. In *The Message* Bible Eugene H.

Peterson wrote, "Every day we wake up in the middle of something that is already going on, that has been going on for a long time—genealogy and geology, history and culture, the cosmos—God. We are neither accidental nor incidental to the story."* You are vital in the life of your family. God knows your genealogy and your place in history, and you were born for such a time as this. He knew your grandchildren before the foundation of the world, and you are "neither accidental nor incidental to the story" of your family.

My grandchildren love to hear about the history of our family. They always think it's really neat when I tell them about the birth and childhood of their mom or dad. Don't ever believe that you are no longer needed. You play a vital role in the lives of your grandchildren.

In each generation God seeks for someone who will build up the wall and stand in the gap before Him for the family, that He should not destroy it. Let it not be said that He "found no one" in your family. You are the bridge from past generations to future generations, and have the opportunity to give guidance and encouragement, teaching your grandchildren about the goodness of God when you spend time with them.

Your prayers will prepare their hearts and minds to receive instruction in wise dealing and the discipline of wise thoughtfulness, righteousness, justice, and integrity.

Pray that each of your grandchildren will hear and increase in learning, acquire skill, and attain to sound counsel so that he may be able to steer his course rightly. (Prov. 1:3-5.)

---

* Peterson, Eugene, *The Message* (NavPress: Colorado Springs, CO), introduction to the book of Matthew.

How To Pray
Prayers That Avail Much®

The prayers in this book are to be used by you for yourself and for your family. They become a matter of the heart when you deliberately pray and meditate on each prayer. Allow the Holy Spirit to make the Word of God a reality in your life. He will cause your spirit to become alive to God's Word, and you will begin thinking as God thinks and talking as He talks even while going about the business of daily living. He will create in you the desire to seek first the Kingdom of God and His righteousness, to read, study, and meditate on the written Word. The Father rewards those who diligently seek Him. (Heb. 11:6.)

Research and contemplate the spiritual significance of each verse listed with the prayers. These are by no means the only Scriptures on certain subjects, but they are a beginning.

These prayers and the study of God's Word will transform your mind and lifestyle. When you are with your grandchildren, you will be ready to give them godly counsel and spiritual guidance with assurance. They are looking for something on which they can depend.

Once you begin delving into God's Word, you must commit to ordering your conversation aright. (Ps. 50:23.)

That is being a doer of the Word. (James 1:22.) Walk in God's counsel, and prize His wisdom. (Ps. 1:1-3,6; Prov. 4:7,8.) Let your heart be fixed and established on God's Word. (Ps. 112.) Then you can point others to that portion of God's Word that is the answer to their problem. Faith always has a good report. (Phil. 4:8.) You cannot pray effectively for yourself, for your grandchildren, or about anything, if you talk negatively about the matter. (Matt. 12:34-37.) To do so is to be double-minded, and a double-minded man cannot expect to receive anything from God. (James 1:6-8.)

In Ephesians 4:29-30 AMP it is written:

Let no foul or polluting language, nor evil word nor unwholesome or worthless talk [ever] come out of your mouth, but only such [speech] as is good and beneficial to the spiritual progress of others, as is fitting to the need and the occasion, that it may be a blessing and give grace (God's favor) to those who hear it.

And do not grieve the Holy Spirit of God [do not offend or vex or sadden Him], by Whom you were sealed (marked, branded as God's own, secured) for the day of redemption (of final deliverance through Christ from evil and the consequences of sin).

Reflect on these words and give them time to bring your perspective into line with God's will. Our Father has much, so very much, to say about that little member, the tongue. (James 3:5-12.) Give the devil no opportunity by getting into worry, unforgiveness, strife, and criticism. Relax with your grandchildren, maintain your sense of humor, and keep your conversation free of idle and foolish talk. (Eph. 4:27,31; 5:4.) Remember that you are to be a blessing to your grandchildren. (Gal. 6:10.)

Talk the answer, not the problem. The answer is in God's Word. To receive that answer, you must have knowledge of the Word—revelation knowledge. (1 Cor. 2:7-16.) The Holy Spirit, your teacher, will reveal the things that have been freely given to us by God. (John 14:26.)

Unite with others in prayer. Consider starting a grandmother's prayer group to pray specifically for each other's grandchildren. United prayer is a mighty weapon. Jesus said, "When two of you get together on anything at all on earth and make a prayer of it, my Father in heaven goes into action. And when two or three of you are together because of me, you can be sure that I'll be there" (Matt. 18:19,20 MESSAGE).

Have faith in God (Mark 11:22), and approach Him confidently. (Heb. 4:16 AMP.) When you pray according to His will, He hears you. Then you know you have what you ask of Him. (1 John 5:14,15 NIV.) "Do not throw away your confidence; it will be richly rewarded." (Heb. 10:35 NIV.) Allow your spirit to pray by the Holy Spirit whose prayers cannot fail. Praise God for the victory now before any manifestation. Walk by faith and not by sight. (2 Cor. 5:7.)

When your faith comes under pressure, don't be moved. As Satan attempts to challenge you, resist him steadfastly in the faith—letting patience have her perfect work. (James 1:4.) Take the sword of the Spirit and the shield of faith and quench his every fiery dart. (Eph. 6:16,17.) The entire substitutionary work of Christ was for you and your family. Satan is now a defeated foe, because Jesus conquered him on the cross. (Col. 2:14,15.) You overcome Satan by the blood of the Lamb and the word of your testimony. (Rev. 12:11.) "Fight the good fight of faith" (1 Tim. 6:12). Withstand the adversary and "be firm in faith [against his onset—rooted, established, strong, immovable, and determined]" (1 Peter 5:9 AMP). Speak God's Word boldly and courageously. (Eph. 6:19.)

Your desire should be to please and to bless the Father. As you pray according to His Word, He joyfully hears that you—His child—are living and walking in the truth. (3 John 1:4.)

How exciting to know that the prayers of the saints are forever in the heavenly throne room! (Rev. 5:7,8.) Hallelujah!

Praise God for His Word and the limitlessness of prayer in the name of Jesus. The privilege of reading and praying the Word in Jesus' name belongs to every child of God. Therefore, run with patience the race that is set before you, looking unto Jesus, the author and finisher of your faith. (Heb. 12:1,2.) God's Word "is able to build you up and to give you [your rightful] inheritance among all God's set-apart ones" (Acts 20:32 AMP).

Commit yourself to pray according to His will, by approaching the throne of God with your mouth filled with His Word!

Effectual Prayer

**...The earnest (heartfelt, continued) prayer
of a righteous man makes tremendous power
available [dynamic in its working].**

James 5:16 AMP

Prayer is fellowship with the Father—vital, personal
contact with God, who is more than enough. (Ps. 4:6
MESSAGE.) We are to be in constant communion with Him:

**For the eyes of the Lord are upon the right-
eous (those who are upright and in right
standing with God), and His ears are attentive to
their prayer....**

1 Peter 3:12 AMP

Prayer is not to be a religious form with no power. It
is to be effective and accurate and bring *results.* God
watches over His Word to perform it. (Jer. 1:12 AMP.)

Prayer that brings results must be based on God's Word.

**For the Word that God speaks is alive and
full of power [making it active, operative, ener-
gizing, and effective]; it is sharper than any two-
edged sword, penetrating to the dividing line of
the breath of life (soul) and [the immortal] spirit,
and of joints and marrow [of the deepest parts of**

**our nature], exposing and sifting and analyzing
and judging the very thoughts and purposes of
the heart.**

Hebrews 4:12 AMP

Prayer is this "living" Word in your mouth. You must speak forth faith, for faith is what pleases God. (Heb. 11:6.) When you hold His Word up to Him in prayer, your Father sees Himself in His Word.

God's Word is your contact with Him. Put Him in remembrance of His Word (Isa. 43:26), asking Him for what you need in the name of Jesus. The woman in Mark 5:25-34 placed a demand on the power of God when she said, "If I can but touch the hem of his garment, I will be healed." (v. 28, author's paraphrase.) By faith she touched His clothes and was healed. You place a demand on the power of God when you declare your faith and expect Him to supply all your need according to His riches in glory by Christ Jesus. (Phil. 4:19.) His Word does not return to Him "void [without producing any effect, useless] but it shall accomplish that which I [God] please and purpose, and it shall prosper in the thing for which I [God] sent it" (Isa. 55:11 AMP). Hallelujah!

You can know God. He did *not* leave you without His thoughts and His ways, for you have His Word—which is His bond. God instructs His children to call upon Him, and He will answer and show them great and mighty things. (Jer. 33:3.) Prayer is to be exciting—not drudgery.

God looks for someone in each generation who will pray for the family. God moves when you pray in faith—believing. He says that His eyes run to and fro throughout the whole earth to show Himself strong in behalf of those whose hearts are blameless toward Him. (2 Chron. 16:9 AMP.) God sees you blameless. (Eph. 1:4 AMP.) You are His very own child. (Eph. 1:5; Gal. 3:26.) You are His righteousness in Christ Jesus. (2 Cor. 5:21.) He invites you to come boldly to the throne of grace and obtain mercy and find grace to help in time of need—appropriate and well-timed help. (Heb. 4:16 AMP.) Praise the Lord!

The prayer armor described in Ephesians 6:11-18 is for every believer, every member of the body of Christ, who will put it on and walk in it. Second Corinthians 10:4 explains why you need to do that: "for the weapons of our warfare are not carnal, but mighty through God to the pulling down of strong holds."

There are many different kinds of prayer, such as the prayer of thanksgiving and praise, the prayer of dedication and worship, and the prayer that changes *things* (not God). Praying God's Word changes you, and you become an instrument of change. All prayer involves a time of fellowshipping with the Father.

Take the sword of the Spirit, which is the Word of
God, and "pray at all times (on every occasion, in every
season) in the Spirit, with all [manner of] prayer and
entreaty" (Eph. 6:18 AMP).

*Prayer is not a suggestion, but the joyful responsibility of
the children of God.* "FIRST OF all, then, I admonish *and*
urge that petitions, prayers, intercessions, and thanksgiv-
ings be offered on behalf of all men" (1 Tim. 2:1 AMP).

The foundation of every Christian endeavor is prayer.
Any failure is a prayer failure. God desires for His people
to be successful, to be filled with a full, deep, and clear
knowledge of His will (His Word), and to bear fruit in
every good work. (Col. 1:9,10 AMP.) You will then bring
honor and glory to Him. (John 15:8.) He desires that you
know how to pray, for "the prayer of the upright is his
delight" (Prov. 15:8).

Your Father has not left you helpless. Not only has He
given you His Word, but He has also given you the Holy
Spirit to help your infirmities when you know not how to
pray as you ought. (Rom. 8:26.) Praise God! Our Father
has provided His people with every possible avenue to
ensure their complete and total victory in this life in the
name of our Lord Jesus. (1 John 5:3-5.)

*Pray to the Father, in the name of Jesus, through the Holy
Spirit, according to the Word!*

Using God's Word on purpose, specifically, in prayer is one means of prayer, and it is a most effective and accurate means. Jesus said, "The words (truths) that I have been speaking to you are spirit and life" (John 6:63 AMP).

When Jesus faced Satan in the wilderness, He said, "It is written...it is written...it is written..." (Matt. 4:4,7,10). Live, be upheld, and be sustained by every word that proceeds from the mouth of God. (v. 4.)

Jesus said in John 15, verse 7: "If you remain in me and my words remain in you, ask whatever you wish, and it will be given you." Keeping God's Word in the midst of your heart is the key to answered prayer. He "is able to do exceedingly abundantly above all that you ask or think, according to the power that works in you" (Eph. 3:20 NKJV). The power lies within God's Word. The Spirit of God does not lead you apart from the Word, for the Word is of the Spirit of God. Apply that Word personally to yourself and to your grandchildren—not adding to or taking from it—in the name of Jesus. Apply the Word to the *now*—to those things, circumstances, and situations you are facing.

Paul was very specific and definite in his praying. The first chapters of Ephesians, Philippians, Colossians, and 2 Thessalonians are examples of how Paul prayed for believers. There are numerous others. *Search them out.* Paul wrote under the inspiration of the Holy Spirit. You can use these Spirit-given prayers today!

In 2 Corinthians 1:11, 2 Corinthians 9:14, and Philippians 1:4 are examples of how believers prayed one for another—putting others first in their prayer life with joy. Faith works by love. (Gal. 5:6.) You will grow spiritually as you reach out to help your grandchildren and others—praying for and with them and holding out to them the Word of life. (Phil. 2:16 AMP.)

Man is a spirit, he has a soul, and he lives in a body. (1 Thess. 5:23.) In order to operate successfully, each of these three parts must be fed properly. The soul, or intellect, feeds on intellectual food to produce intellectual strength. The body feeds on physical food to produce physical strength. The spirit—the heart, or inward man— is the real person, the part that has been reborn in Christ Jesus. It must feed on spiritual food, which is God's Word, in order to produce and develop faith. As you feast upon God's Word, your mind becomes renewed with His Word, and you have "a fresh mental and spiritual attitude" (Eph. 4:23,24 AMP).

Likewise, you are to present your body "a living sacrifice, holy, acceptable unto God" (Rom. 12:1). So do not let your body dominate you, but bring it into subjection to your spirit man. (1 Cor. 9:27; Eph. 3:16; 1 Peter 3:4.) God's Word is healing and health to all your flesh. (Prov.

4:22 AMP.) Therefore, God's Word affects each part of your being—spirit, soul, and body. You become vitally united to the Father, to Jesus, and to the Holy Spirit—one with each Person of the Holy Trinity. (John 16:13-15; John 17:20-22; Col. 2:6-10.)

Purpose to hear, accept, and welcome the Word, and it will take root within your spirit and save your soul. Believe the Word, speak the Word, and act on the Word—it is a creative force. The Word is sharper than a double-edged sword. (Heb. 4:12.) Often it places a demand on you to change attitudes and behaviors toward your children, children-in-law, and grandchildren for whom you are praying.

"Be doers of the word, and not hearers only, deceiving yourselves" (James 1:22 NKJV). Faith without works, or corresponding actions, is dead. (James 2:17 AMP.) Don't be like the mental assenters—those who agree that the Bible is true but who never act on it. *Real faith is acting on God's Word now.* You cannot build faith without practicing the Word. You cannot develop an effective prayer life that is anything but empty words unless God's Word actually has a part in your life. Hold fast to your confession of the Word's truthfulness. (Heb. 10:23.) The Lord Jesus is "the High Priest of your confession" (Heb. 3:1 NKJV), and He is "the Guarantee of a better (stronger) agreement [a more excellent and more advantageous covenant]" (Heb. 7:22 AMP).

Prayer does not cause faith to work, but faith causes prayer to work. Therefore, any prayer problem is the result of a lack of knowledge, a wrong motive, or the presence of doubt—doubt in the integrity of the Word and the ability of God to stand behind His promises or the statements of fact in the Word.

You can spend fruitless hours in prayer if your heart is not prepared beforehand. Preparation of the heart, the spirit, comes from meditation in the Father's Word: meditation on who you are in Christ, what He is to you, and what the Holy Spirit can mean to you as you become God-inside minded. Just as God told Joshua, as you meditate on the Word day and night and do according to all that is written in it, then you will make your way prosperous and have good success. (Josh. 1:8.) Attend to God's Word, submit to His sayings, keep them in the center of your heart, and put far away from you any false, dishonest, willful, and contrary talk. (Prov. 4:20-24 AMP.)

The Holy Spirit is a divine Helper (John 14:26 AMP), and He will direct your prayer and help you pray when you don't know how. (Rom. 8:26.) When you use God's Word in prayer, this is *not* something you just rush through, uttering once. Do *not* be mistaken. There is nothing "magical" nor "manipulative" about it—no set pattern or device in order to satisfy selfish desires. Instead, you are holding God's Word before Him. Jesus said to ask the Father in His name. (John 15:16.)

Expect God's divine intervention while you choose not to look at the things that are seen, but at the things that are unseen, for the things that are seen are subject to change. (2 Cor. 4:18.)

Effective prayer ensues from an intimate relationship with the Father and is based upon the Word, which rises above the senses, contacts the Author of the Word, and sets His spiritual laws into motion. It is not just saying prayers that gets results, but it is spending time with the Father, learning His wisdom, drawing on His strength, being filled with His quietness, and basking in His love that bring results to our prayers. Praise the Lord!

* * *

The prayers in this book are designed to teach and train you in the art of prayer. As you pray them, you will be reinforcing the prayer armor, which we have been instructed to put on. (Eph. 6:11.) The material from which the armor is made is the Word of God. Live by every word that proceeds from the mouth of God. (Luke 4:4.) Desire the whole counsel of God. By receiving that counsel, you will be "...transformed (changed) by the [entire] renewal of your mind [by its new ideals and its new attitude], so that you may prove [for yourselves] what is the good and acceptable and perfect will of God, even the thing which is good and acceptable and perfect [in His sight for you]" (Rom. 12:2 AMP).

The Personal Prayers in Part 3 may be used as intercessory prayer by simply praying them in the third person, changing the pronouns *I* or *we* to the name of the person for whom you are interceding and then adjusting the pronouns and verbs accordingly. The Holy Spirit is your Helper. Remember that you cannot control another's will, but your prayers can prepare the hearts of your grandchildren to hear, receive, and understand truth.

An often-asked question is this: "How many times should I pray the same prayer?"

The answer is simple: You pray until you know that the answer is fixed in your heart. After that, you need to repeat the prayer whenever adverse circumstances or long delays cause you to be tempted to doubt that your prayer has been heard and your request granted. Let patience have full play and do a perfect work!

The Word of God is your weapon against the temptation to lose heart and grow weary in your prayer life. (2 Thess. 3:13.) When that Word of promise becomes fixed in your heart, you will find yourself praising, giving glory to God for the answer, even when the only evidence you have of that answer is your own faith. Reaffirming your faith with praise and thanksgiving enforces the triumphant victory of our Lord Jesus Christ.

Another question often asked is this: "When we repeat prayers more than once, aren't we praying 'vain repetitions'?"

Obviously, such people are referring to the admonition of Jesus when He told His disciples: "And when you pray, do not heap up phrases (multiply words, repeating the same ones over and over) as the Gentiles do, for they think they will be heard for their much speaking" (Matt. 6:7 AMP). Praying the Word of God is not praying the kind of prayer that the "heathen" pray. You will note in 1 Kings 18:25-29 the manner of prayer that was offered to the gods who could not hear. That is not the way you and I pray. The words that we speak are not vain, but they are spirit and life. (John 6:63.) You have a God whose eyes are over the righteous and whose ears are open to His children (Ps. 34:15): When you pray, He hears you. (1 John 5:14,15.)

You are the righteousness of God in Christ Jesus (1 Cor. 1:30), and your prayers will avail much. (James 5:16.) They will bring salvation to the sinner, deliverance to the oppressed, healing to the sick, and prosperity to the poor. They will usher in the next move of God on the earth. In addition to affecting outward circumstances and other people, your prayers will also affect you.

By the very process of praying, your life will be changed as you go from faith to faith (Rom. 1:17) and from glory to glory. (2 Cor. 3:18.)

As a Christian, your first priority is to love the Lord your God with your entire being, and your neighbor as yourself. (Mark 12:30,31.) You are called to be an intercessor, a man or woman of prayer. (1 Tim. 2:1.) You are to seek the face of the Lord as you inquire, listen, meditate, and consider in the temple of the Lord. (Ps. 27:4 AMP.)

Because you are one of "God's set-apart ones" (Acts 20:32 AMP), the will of the Lord for your life is the same as it is for the life of every other true believer: "Seek ye first the kingdom of God, and his righteousness; and all these things shall be added unto you" (Matt. 6:33).

Personal Declarations

Dear Grandparent:

Speaking the following personal declarations will establish who you are in Christ Jesus and prepare you to pray with confidence and power.

Now glory be to God, who by his mighty power at work within us is able to do far more than we would ever dare to ask or even dream of—infinitely beyond our highest prayers, desires, thoughts, or hopes.

Ephesians 3:20 TLB

Declarations of Faith

Jesus is Lord over my spirit, my soul, and my body. (Phil. 2:9-11.)

Jesus has been made unto me wisdom, righteousness, sanctification, and redemption. I can do all things through Christ, who strengthens me. (1 Cor. 1:30; Phil. 4:13 NKJV.)

The Lord is my Shepherd. I do not want. My God supplies all my need according to His riches in glory in Christ Jesus. (Ps. 23:1; Phil. 4:19.)

I do not fret or have anxiety about anything. I do not have a care. (Phil. 4:6 AMP; 1 Peter 5:6,7.)

I am the body of Christ. I am redeemed from the
curse, because Jesus bore my sicknesses and carried my
diseases in His own body. By His stripes I am healed. I
forbid any sickness or disease to operate in my body.
Every organ, every tissue of my body, functions in the
perfection in which God created it to function. I honor
God and bring glory to Him in my body. (Gal. 3:13;
Matt. 8:17 NIV; 1 Peter 2:24; 1 Cor. 6:20 AMP.)

I have the mind of Christ and hold the thoughts, feelings, and purposes of His heart. (1 Cor. 2:16 AMP.)

I am a believer and not a doubter. I hold fast to my
confession of faith. I decide to walk by faith and practice
faith. My faith comes by hearing, and hearing by the
Word of God. Jesus is the author, developer, and finisher
of my faith. (Heb. 4:14 NKJV; Heb. 11:6; Rom. 10:17 NKJV;
Heb. 12:2.)

The Holy Spirit has shed the love of God abroad in
my heart, and His love abides in me richly. I keep myself
in the kingdom of light, in love, in the Word; and the
wicked one touches me not. (Rom. 5:5; 1 John 4:16;
1 Tim. 6:17; 1 John 5:18.)

I tread upon serpents and scorpions and have power
over all the power of the enemy. I take my shield of faith
and quench his every fiery dart. Greater is He who is in
me than he who is in the world. (Luke 10:19; Eph. 6:16;
1 John 4:4 NKJV.)

I am delivered from this present evil world. I am seated with Christ in heavenly places far above principalities, powers, might and dominion, and every name that is named not only in this world but also in that which is to come. I reside in the kingdom of God's dear Son. The law of the Spirit of life in Christ Jesus has made me free from the law of sin and death. (Gal. 1:4; Eph. 2:6; Col. 1:13; Rom. 8:2.)

I fear not, for God has given me a spirit of power, and of love, and of a sound mind. God is on my side. (2 Tim. 1:7; Rom. 8:31 AMP.)

I hear the voice of the Good Shepherd. I hear my Father's voice, and the voice of a stranger I will not follow. I roll my works upon the Lord. I commit and trust them wholly to Him. He will cause my thoughts to become agreeable to His will, and so shall my plans be established and succeed. (John 10:1-5,11,14,27; Prov. 16:3 AMP.)

I am a world-overcomer because I am born of God. I represent the Father and Jesus well. I am a useful member in the body of Christ. I am His workmanship re-created in Christ Jesus. My God is all the while effectually at work in me both to will and to work for His good pleasure. (1 John 5:4,5; 2 Cor. 5:20 AMP; Eph. 2:10 AMP; Phil. 2:13 AMP.)

I let the Word dwell in me richly. He who began a good work in me will continue until the day of Christ. (Col. 3:16; Phil. 1:6 AMP.)

I love the Lord my God with all my heart, and with all my soul, and with all my mind, and I love my neighbor as myself. (Matt. 22:37-39.)

Part 1

Prayers for Grandparenting

To Bring Honor to God as a Grandparent

Father, I come before You today with an offering of praise and thanksgiving so that I may honor and glorify You in all my relationships. I pray that in every relationship I will order my way of life with integrity [speaking truly, dealing truly, and living truly] for Your glory and honor.

Father, Your love is shed abroad in my heart by the Holy Spirit, and I rely on Him to help me love my grandchildren with unconditional love. As occasion permits I will reinforce the training, teaching, nurturing, and godly admonition of their parents.

In my family I purpose to do everything in the name of Jesus and in [dependence] upon His Person. I will endeavor to fulfill my responsibility to You and my grandchildren as [something done] for You and not for men. To You, Father, be all glory and honor and praise.

In the name of Jesus I pray. Amen.

Scripture References

Psalm 50:23 AMP

Romans 5:5

Colossians 3:17 AMP

Ephesians 4:15 AMP

Ephesians 6:4

Colossians 3:23

Grandparents Raising Their Grandchildren

Dear Grandparent:

When you have to take full responsibility for the continuous care of your grandchildren, it is not in the natural order of things. Once again, you become parents, and your first responsibility is to keep your grandchildren safe, while also seeing to their spiritual, physical, mental, and emotional development. You have to set boundaries and manage them at all times, even in painful situations.

Prayer

Father, hear my heart's cry. You knew these grandchildren and me before the foundation of the world. I am in an uncomfortable place, and I need Your help, Your divine energy, just to get through every day. I rely on Your grace, which is more than enough, to walk in humility, with dignity and nobility before my grandchildren.

In the name of Jesus, I bind my mind to the mind of Christ; I bind my will, purposes, and plans to Yours, my Father. I loose unforgiveness, resentment, bad feelings toward others, wrong attitudes, and perceptions from my mind; and I bind my emotions to the control of the Holy Spirit. I bind my thoughts, attitudes, and behavior to the fruit of the Spirit. I accept this responsibility because You are my God, and I trust You to be my help in every situation.

In the name Jesus, I allow these little children to come to me. All authority (all power of rule) in heaven and on earth has been given to You, and I will make disciples of my grandchildren, teaching them to observe everything that You have commanded me. You are with me on every occasion. Each and every day I accept and receive and welcome these children into my heart and my home.

I ask for the parenting skills that will help me train up each child in the way he/she should go [and in keeping with his/her individual gift or bent], and when he/she is old he/she will not depart from it.

Thank You for supplying my every need—spiritually, physically, mentally, emotionally, and financially—for the good and benefit of these grandchildren. Thank You for the support of my church, family, and friends. Most of all, I rest knowing that You will never leave me or forsake me.

In the name of Jesus, I pray.

Scripture References

Ephesians 1:4

Matthew 18:18

Galatians 5:22,23

Matthew 28:18-20

John 10:10

Philippians 4:19

2 Corinthians 12:9

1 Corinthians 2:16

Luke 18:16 AMP

Proverbs 22:6

Romans 8:28

Hebrews 18:5

To Have the Answers to Your Grandchildren's Questions

Dear Grandparent:

You may be grieving over the death of a son or daughter, or angry and saddened by your adult child who has made poor choices and can no longer raise the children, or disappointed by your teenager whose sexual indiscretion has turned your world upside down. Your grandchildren need honest answers to difficult, troubling questions. God will help you answer these questions with love and grace. Validate and affirm them as intelligent children of the Most High God.

Prayer

O, my Father, I come into Your throne room asking for mercy and grace. Behold, You desire truth in the inward parts; in the hidden part You will make me to know wisdom. Your wisdom will enable me to be straightforward, answering my grandchildren's questions openly and honestly in love.

O Lord, God of Abraham, Isaac, and Israel, let it be known today that You are God in our family, and that I am Your servant. Answer me, O Lord; answer me, so that my grandchildren will know that You, O Lord, are God. I pray that they will know and proclaim, "The Lord—He is God! The Lord—He is God!" (1 Kings 18:39 NIV).

My grandchildren are distressed about this present situation. Lord, help me answer them and give them assurance that You will protect and guide them, that you will never leave or forsake them. I bind their spirits, souls, and bodies to Your love and mercy. In the name of Jesus I loose shame and self-condemnation from them. They are not responsible for the mistakes their parents have made.* I ask for Your wisdom to give me the answers my grandchildren need.

Thank You for Your grace, which is sufficient to give me a gentle answer that turns away wrath. As a man/woman in right standing with You, I will weigh my answers. My conversation will be full of grace, seasoned with salt, so that I may know how to answer my grandchildren with gentleness.

It is in the name of Jesus that I pray. Amen.

Scripture References

Psalm 51:6 NKJV

1 Kings 18:36-39 NIV

Psalm 20:1

Proverbs 10:19 NKJV

Proverbs 15:1 NKJV

Proverbs 15:28 NIV

Colossians 4:6 NIV

---

* This applies to parents who are absent because of addictions, severe emotional problems, incarceration, or other unfit situations. Often children even blame themselves for the death of a parent. In today's environment military parents may be absent not by choice but because they have been called to active duty. In some cases, a parent may be medically unable to care for the children. Your grandchildren will need your help as they resolve feelings of bewilderment and abandonment.

Maintaining Good Relations
With Your Grandchildren

Father, in the name of Jesus, I will not withhold any good thing from my grandchildren when it is in the power of my hand to help them fulfill their destinies. I will not lose heart, grow weary, or faint in acting nobly and doing right toward them, for in due season I shall reap if I do not loosen and relax my courage or faint. I resist the temptation to judge or condemn them. I will be slow to speak and quick to listen, that I may have understanding.

So then, as occasion and opportunity open up to me, I will do good to these who are so dear to me [not only being useful or profitable to them, but also doing what is for their spiritual good and advantage]. I will be an example to my grandchildren by being a blessing and by helping others.

I will not contend with my grandchildren for no reason but will seek to speak to them with respect, extending grace and mercy on every occasion. Give me the wisdom to offer encouragement and guidance. If possible, as far as it depends on me, I purpose to live at peace with everyone. Amen.

Scripture References

Proverbs 3:27 AMP

Romans 13:7 AMP

Galatians 6:9,10 AMP

Proverbs 3:30 AMP

Romans 12:18 AMP

Grandparenting With Wisdom

Father, I come before Your throne of grace asking for wisdom that is pure, peace-loving, considerate, submissive, full of mercy and good fruit, impartial, and sincere. Thank You for giving me wisdom, and the grace to be single-minded, stable in all my ways with and for my grandchildren.

Lord, from Your mouth come knowledge and understanding, and I thank You for teaching me wisdom in the inmost place. I declare and decree that my mouth will speak words of wisdom; the utterance from my heart will give understanding. If I am wise when I instruct and correct my grandchildren, wisdom will reward me.

I desire to be a wise grandfather/grandmother who is discerning; one who speaks pleasant words that promote instruction. My spirit will guide my mouth, and my lips will promote instruction. Give me the grace to be quick to listen, slow to speak, and slow to anger. Jesus has been made unto me wisdom, and I will keep myself in the love of God, binding my emotions to the control of the Holy Spirit.

Father, forgive me for the times I have spoken to my grandchildren without thinking. I purpose to guide my grandchildren with patience and resist the temptation to indulge them. Thank You for hearing my prayer, in the name of Jesus. Amen.

Scripture References

James 1:5 NIV

Proverbs 2:6

Psalm 49:3

Proverbs 16:21-23 NIV

1 Corinthians 1:30

James 3:17 AMP

Psalm 51:6

Proverbs 9:10-12 NIV

James 1:19 AMP

Finances

Father, I come before You concerning the added expenses of parenting our grandchildren. I reverently fear You, my Lord. You are my help and my shield, and You are mindful of us. You daily load us with benefits, and You will increase me and my grandchildren more and more.

On the authority of Your Word I am confident that You will take care of everything we need; Your generosity exceeds mine in the glory that pours from Jesus. We will have everything we need and plenty left over to share with others.

God, You are able to make all grace (every favor and earthly blessing) come to us in abundance so that we may always, and under all circumstances and whatever the need, be self-sufficient [possessing enough to require no aid or support and furnished in abundance for every good work and charitable donation].

Thank You for hearing my prayer and watching over Your Word to perform it, in the name of Jesus.

Scripture References

Psalm 115:11-14 AMP   Psalm 68:19

Philippians 4:19 MESSAGE   2 Corinthians 9:8 NLT, AMP

Leaving Grandchildren a Spiritual Inheritance

Dear Grandparent:

Granddads and grandmothers like Lois in the Bible (see 2 Tim. 1:5) can serve as spiritual models for their grandchildren as they daily demonstrate the reality of walking with God through good as well as tough times. Whether we're aware of it or not, we are continually in the process of creating a legacy that will be passed on to our grandchildren and the generations to follow.*

I am so thankful for my parents, Rev. A. H. "Buck" and Donnis Brock Griffin, who left their children and grandchildren a legacy of joy, faith in God, and prayer that avails much.

Prayer

Father, thank You for the grace and peace You have given me. You have blessed me with all spiritual blessings in Christ Jesus, and I pray that my grandchildren will receive the spiritual inheritance, which is their real reward. May they know that the One whom I actually serve is the Lord Jesus Christ, my elder Brother, my Messiah.

Lord, You are my chosen and assigned portion, my cup; You hold and maintain my lot. The lines have fallen for me in pleasant places; yes, I have a good heritage to pass on to my children and their children.

I pray that my grandchildren will keep their father's (and grandfather's) [God-given] commandment and forsake not the law of [God] taught by their mother (and grandmother). In the name of Jesus, I bind Your words upon their hearts and tie them about their necks. When they go, they [the words of their parents and grandparents] shall lead them; when they sleep, they shall keep them; and when they waken, they shall talk with You.

O God, You have helped me from my earliest childhood—and I have constantly testified to others of the wonderful things You do. And now that I am old and gray, don't forsake me. Give me time to tell this new generation (and their children too) about all Your mighty miracles.

Scripture References

Ephesians 1	Colossians 3:24
Proverbs 16:5,6 AMP	Proverbs 6:20-22
Psalm 71:17,18 TLB	

---

* Excerpt from Ruthanne Garlock and Quin M. Sherrer's *Grandma, I Need Your Prayers—Blessing Your Grandchildren Through the Power of Prayer* (Grand Rapids, Michigan: Zondervan, 2002).

Understanding Boundaries

Dear Grandparent:

It is important that we understand boundaries and avoid building walls that separate and divide families. Your adult children are responsible for "working out their own salvation with fear and trembling" (Phil. 2:12) and defining their methods of parenting. As grandparents we must learn where our responsibility begins and ends.

My husband and I learned many painful lessons when we became grandparents for the first time. We had to learn to make suggestions, allow our children to make their own decisions, and let go of the consequences. We can't change others, but with God's help we can change ourselves. Grandparents have much wisdom to share, but there is a time and place for all things.

My mother was very wise. She reinforced the standards and values my husband and I established for our children and expressed her concerns about some of our parenting methods with me in private, pointing out where we were too harsh or too lenient. She talked to me about the importance of supplying their basic needs and made helpful suggestions. To this day I appreciate her sensitivity and her wise counsel.

Where boundary lines are fuzzy, communication breaks down. However, prayer will clear the way for the will of God to be done in the lives of your grandchildren. God spoke to me on an occasion when I was obsessing about perceived mistakes my children were making with my grandchildren, "Germaine, I was bigger than your mistakes. I am bigger than theirs." Let go and let God.

Prayer

Father, to everything there is a season, and a time to every purpose under heaven. Each season requires a shift in boundaries, and I need wisdom to know when to keep silent and when to speak to my children about my concerns for my grandchildren. Grant me the grace to be patient so I can make allowances for them because we love one another. In the name of Jesus I bind Your Word upon our hearts that we might be eager and strive earnestly to guard and keep the harmony and oneness of the Spirit in the binding power of peace.

Teach me to keep and guard my heart (set boundaries) with all vigilance; above all I guard my heart, for out of it flow the springs of life. I loose manipulative and controlling thought patterns and behaviors from my mind; I put away false and dishonest speech and willful and contrary talk. My trust is in You, and in the name of Jesus I set boundaries and let go of the outcome.

Teach me to respect the wishes and desires of my children and grandchildren. I will do nothing from factional motives through manipulation, contentiousness, strife, and selfishness. I will not be merely concerned with my own interests, but also with the interests of my children and grandchildren. I will not undermine the authority of my children by allowing my grandchildren to do things they have been told they cannot do, even when I disagree.

I will express truth with my children and grandchildren, telling them how I feel without accusation, and set boundaries that are flexible. I purpose to speak the truth in love, and to avoid inappropriate behavior that would be detrimental to the welfare of my family. I will impart wisdom when asked and refrain from judging and criticizing the parents of my grandchildren, in the name of Jesus.

Scripture References

Ecclesiastes 3:1   Ephesians 4:4 AMP
Proverbs 4:23 AMP   Philippians 2:3,4 AMP
Matthew 7:1 AMP

Prayer for Children To Be Good Parents

Father, I bring my children who are now parents before You, asking You to give them strength and wisdom for the task before them. They are not sufficient of themselves, but their sufficiency is of You. In every situation help them to remember that Your grace is sufficient; Your strength is made perfect in weakness.

Father, my grandchildren are prone to foolishness and fads. I ask You to give their parents the grace to apply the cure that comes through tough-minded, loving discipline.

In the name of Jesus I bind their minds to the mind of Christ, and their emotions to the control of the Holy Spirit. Daily, cause Your Word to rise up within them as they teach and train these grandchildren. Holy Spirit, I ask You to remind them that they are not to provoke and exasperate their children with abusive language or harsh physical treatment, but they are to nurture, correct, and instruct them in the ways of righteousness.

My children and their children belong to You, and the law of kindness is in their hearts and in their mouths. May these parents resist the temptation to make idle, unproductive threats. Teach them through wise counsel, teaching tapes, and/or books to set boundaries of protection and security for their children. I bind their plans and purposes to Your plans and purposes so they will train the children up in the way they should go.

Holy Spirit, cause the Word of God that is in their hearts to rise up just when they need to hear from heaven. I declare and decree, in the name of Jesus, that they will teach the ways of God to their children and talk of them when they walk by the way, when they lie down, and when they rise up. Thank You for sending the Holy Spirit to be their helper, comforter, strengthener, and standby.

Father, I pray that these parents will be imitators of You, shepherding their children with love. Thank You for giving them the grace to lead their children into paths of righteousness for Your name's sake.

Thank You for watching over and performing Your Word in the lives of my children and grandchildren each and every day. Amen.

Scripture References

Psalm 27:10	Philippians 2:4 AMP
2 Corinthians 3:5	Deuteronomy 6:7 AMP
2 Corinthians 12:9	John 14:16 AMP
Proverbs 22:15 MESSAGE	James 3:17 AMP
Ephesians 6:4 AMP	Colossians 1:13 MESSAGE
Proverbs 31:26	James 3

Proverbs 22:6

Ephesians 6:1-4

Proverbs 13:24 MESSAGE

1 Peter 5:1-4 AMP

2 Corinthians 10:12

1 Corinthians 13:11 AMP

Psalm 23:3

Jeremiah 1:12 AMP

Bridging the Generational Gap

by Janet Blackwell
Member of the Word Ministries Prayer Team

O God, how good You are to me. Thank You for
giving me the opportunity to bless my children, grandchildren, and great-grandchildren. I will bless these
generations in my path with the testimony of Your goodness and grace.

You have not forsaken me at any stage of my life.
Instead, Father, You have allowed me to experience victory
in Jesus with each and every trial and tribulation. I have
learned the source of my ever-present help. You are my
hope, my deliverer. I will declare Your strength to the next
generation, Your power to everyone who is to come.

Teach me, Father, to convey the commandments of
Your Word through Your love and gentleness. Instead of
causing division with judgments, let me bridge the generational gaps with unconditional love, with Your truth and
Your promises. Where there are mistakes, impatience,
and offense, Lord, bring healing, encouragement, and
redemption. I am in awe that You continue to use me,
even in my human weaknesses, to put Your arms around
my grandchildren and their friends. I yield all my
thoughts, plans, attitudes, and expectations to You, Father,

about my role in the lives of these grandchildren and
great-grandchildren. I commit to fight the good fight of
faith on my assigned battlefield. As opportunities arise, I
will teach my precious grandchildren how to follow the
steps of good men and stay on the paths of righteousness.
They need to know that only the upright will live in the
land and those who have integrity will remain in it. How
will they know this integrity lest they see it first in me?

I will not hide these truths, but will tell the next
generation about the glorious deeds of my Lord. I will tell
of Your power and the mighty miracles Jesus did. As I do,
they will learn of our Father's open arms, which are always
eager for a wayward one's return.

Praise You, God, that You silence our accuser and cast
our failures into the sea of forgetfulness. In Your gracious-
ness You have allowed me to close the doors of generational sin that the enemy would have used against my
children and their children. You promise that if we confess
our sins, You are faithful and just to forgive us our sins
and to cleanse us from all unrighteousness.

Every generation, Lord, is entitled to fullness of life in
Christ Jesus. How precious is this forgiveness from generation to generation. I will tell of my own deliverance
because I am standing on the solid rock. I will not leave
one behind, but will continually declare the goodness of
my God. Through family, friendships, and associations,

Father, You have linked our destinies across decades. Your Word shall not depart from my mouth, nor from the mouth of my descendants from this time on, through eternity. Your Spirit will touch the lives of those in my sphere of influence. My joy in You will be full as I am filled with Your Holy Spirit, speaking to the next generations in psalms and hymns and spiritual songs, singing and making melody in my heart to the Lord. Father, You have filled my mouth with laughter, and I thank You for giving me a sense of humor that helps bridge any generational gap.

Praise God, Your way works! Praise God, I am neither alone nor left behind, for I am about the business of the King. Praise God, the silver-haired head is a crown of glory if it is found in the way of righteousness. I hear You and shall love You, the Lord my God, with all my heart, with all my soul, and with all my might. Lord, may I finish my assignment and be a living memorial to show my future generations that the Lord is upright and faithful to His promises.

Scripture References

Psalm 71:18 NKJV

Psalm 78:4 NLT

Isaiah 59:21

Proverbs 16:31 NKJV

Proverbs 2:20,21 NLT

1 John 1:9 NKJV

Ephesians 5:18

Deuteronomy 6:5,7 NKJV

Part 2

PRAYERS FOR YOUR GRANDCHILDREN

The Grandchildren

Father, in the name of Jesus, I pray and confess Your Word over my grandchildren and surround them with my faith—faith in You and Your Word. My heart overflows with thanksgiving because You are watching over Your Word to perform it! I confess and believe that my grandchildren are disciples of Christ, taught of the Lord and obedient to Your will. Great is the peace and undisturbed composure of my grandchildren because You contend with that which contends with my grandchildren; You give them safety and ease them day by day.

Father, You will perfect that which concerns me. I commit and cast the care of my grandchildren over on You. They are in Your hands, and I am positively persuaded that You are able to guard and keep that which I commit to You. You are more than enough!

In the name of Jesus, I ask You to energize and create within my grandchildren the power and desire, both to will and to work for Your good pleasure, satisfaction, *and* delight, that they may obey their parents in the Lord as Your representatives because this is just and right. May they _____ (name them) always honor, esteem, and value as precious their parents, for this is the first commandment with a promise: that all may be well with them and that they may live long on the earth. They will choose life and love You, Lord, obey Your voice, and cling to You; for You are their life and the length of their days. Therefore, my grandchildren are the head and not the tail, and they shall be above only and not beneath. They are blessed when they come in and when they go out.

Thank You for giving Your angels charge over my grandchildren to accompany and defend and preserve them in all their ways. You, Lord, are their refuge and fortress. You are their glory and the lifter of their heads.

O Lord, my Lord, how excellent (majestic and glorious) is Your name in all the earth! You have set Your glory above the heavens. Out of the mouth of babes and nursing infants You have established strength because of Your foes, that You might silence the enemy and the avenger. I sing praises to Your name, O Most High. The enemy is turned back from my grandchildren, in the name of Jesus! My grandchildren are increasing in wisdom and in favor with God and man. Amen.

Scripture References

Jeremiah 1:12	Psalm 91:11
Isaiah 54:13	Psalm 91:2
Isaiah 49:25	Psalm 3:3
1 Peter 5:7	Colossians 3:21
2 Timothy 1:12	Ephesians 6:4

Ephesians 6:1-3   Proverbs 22:6

Deuteronomy 30:19,20   Psalm 8:1,2

Deuteronomy 28:13   Psalm 9:2,3

Deuteronomy 28:3,6   Luke 2:52

The Home

Dear Grandparent:

Pray for the salvation of any unsaved children and their spouses. After you have prayed, believe and give glory to God for their salvation, and expect to see a performance of His will in the lives of your children and grandchildren.

Prayer

Father, I thank You that You have blessed my children and their families with all spiritual blessings in Christ Jesus.

Through skillful and godly wisdom are their houses (their lives, homes, and families) built, and by understanding they are established on a sound and good foundation. By knowledge shall their chambers be filled with all precious and pleasant riches—great, priceless treasure. The house of the uncompromisingly righteous shall stand; prosperity and welfare are in their houses, in the name of Jesus.

My children's and grandchildren's houses are securely built and founded on a rock—revelation knowledge of Your Word, Father. Jesus is their cornerstone. Jesus is Lord of their households. In the name of Jesus, I bind my children's and grandchildren's spirits, souls, and bodies to the will and purposes of God for their lives.

They love each other with the God-kind of love and dwell in peace. Their homes are deposited into Your charge, entrusted to Your protection and care.

Amen.

Scripture References

Ephesians 1:3	Acts 4:11
Proverbs 24:3,4 AMP	Acts 16:31
Proverbs 15:6	Philippians 2:10,11
Proverbs 12:7 AMP	Colossians 3:23
Psalm 112:3	Colossians 3:14,15
Luke 6:48	Acts 20:32

Blessing the Household

Dear Grandparent:

Jesus Christ, the faithful and true witness, has formed you to be a priest to His God and Father. (Rev. 1:6,7 AMP.) Today, even as in the Old Testament, we are to bear the names of our family members upon our shoulders as a memorial before the Lord. (Ex. 28:12.) As grandparents, we have the privilege and spiritual responsibility to pray for our children and grandchildren.

Build a legacy of faith in God, and blessings will flow from generation to generation. "The mercy and loving-kindness of the Lord are from everlasting to everlasting upon those who reverently and worshipfully fear Him, and His righteousness is to children's children—to such as keep His covenant [hearing, receiving, loving, and obeying it] and to those who [earnestly] remember His command-ments to do them [imprinting them on their hearts]" (Ps. 103:17-28 AMP).

When your children and their children are sitting around your dinner table, I encourage you to pray bless-ings over them individually.

In today's society, grandparents often find themselves needing to make room for adult children and/or their children, and sometimes taking full responsibility for the grandchildren. If you find yourself in one of these situations, keep in mind that under the leadership of the Holy Spirit you are the spiritual authority in your home, and pray as such.

I.

Prayer of Blessing
for the Household

Father, as the priest and head of this household, I declare and decree, "As for me and my house, we shall serve the Lord."

Praise be to You, the God and Father of our Lord Jesus Christ, for You have blessed us in the heavenly realms with every spiritual blessing in Christ. We reverence You and worship You in spirit and in truth.

Lord, we acknowledge and welcome the presence of Your Holy Spirit here in our home. We thank You, Father, that Your Son, Jesus, is here with us because we are gathered together in His name.

Lord God, Your divine power has given us everything we need for life and godliness through our knowledge of You. You have called us by Your own glory and goodness.

As spiritual leader of this home, I declare on the authority of Your Word that my family will be mighty in the land; this generation of the upright will be blessed.

Father, You delight in the prosperity of Your people; and we thank You that wealth and riches are in our house and that our righteousness endures forever.

In the name of Jesus I pray. Amen.

Scripture References

Revelation 1:6	Matthew 18:20
Joshua 24:15	2 Peter 1:3 NIV
Ephesians 1:3 NIV	Psalm 112:2 NIV
John 4:23	Psalm 112:3

II.

Prayer of Blessing at the Table

Dear Grandparent:

This prayer was written for the head of the household to pray not only to thank and praise God for His blessings, but also to cleanse and consecrate the food received and to sanctify the family members who partake of it. I encourage you to take your place as the patriarch or matriarch of your household and bless the Father, who gives us our daily bread.

Prayer

Father, thank You for giving to us our daily bread. We receive this food with thanksgiving and praise. You bless our bread and our water and take sickness out of the midst of us.

In the name of Jesus, we call this food clean, wholesome, and pure nourishment to our bodies. Should there be any deadly thing herein, it shall not harm us, for the Spirit of life in Christ Jesus makes us free from the law of sin and death.

In the name of Jesus I pray. Amen.

Scripture References

Matthew 6:11	Mark 16:18
1 Timothy 4:4 NIV	Romans 8:2
Exodus 23:25	

III.

Grandfather's Prayer of Blessing for His Wife

Dear Grandparent:

It is positive reinforcement, validation, and affirmation for grandchildren to hear their grandfather pray, blessing his wife and their grandmother. This is a method of honoring her and reaffirming her position in the family. Words are powerful, and the blessing for your wife in front of the grandchildren affirms her and validates her place in the family structure. This builds in them a positive self-esteem necessary for success in life.

Sometimes a grandmother will feel that she has failed because she is not fulfilling all the roles expressed in Proverbs 31. I believe that God had this passage written to encourage a woman to be all that He created her to be. Out of her "being"—knowing herself, both her strengths and her weaknesses, developing her talents, seeing herself as God sees her, and looking to Christ for her completeness (wholeness)—comes the "doing."

The *Life Application Bible*, New International Version edition, adds this commentary to the subject:

> The woman described in this chapter has outstanding abilities. Her family's social position is high. In fact, she may not be one woman at all—she may be a composite portrait of ideal womanhood. Do not see her as a model to imitate in every detail; your days are not long enough to do everything she does! See her instead as an inspiration to be all you can be. We can't be just like her, but we can learn from her industry, integrity, and resourcefulness.[2]

Prayer

Father, I thank You for my wife, who is now a mother and grandmother. She is a capable, intelligent, virtuous (valiant) woman, and her worth is far more precious than jewels, and her value is far above rubies or pearls.

I thank You that she is a woman of strong character, great wisdom, many skills, and great compassion. Strength and dignity are her clothing, and her position in this family is strong and secure. She opens her mouth with skillful and godly wisdom, and on her tongue is the law of kindness [giving counsel and instruction].

Our children and grandchildren rise up and call her blessed (happy, fortunate, and to be envied); and I boast of and praise her, [saying], "Many daughters have done virtuously, nobly, and well [with the strength of character that is steadfast in goodness], but you excel them all."

Father, my wife reverently and worshipfully fears You; she shall be praised! Give her of the fruit of her hands, and let her own works praise her in the gates [of the city].

Today and every day I respect, value, and honor my wife before our children and grandchildren.

In the name of Jesus I pray. Amen.

Scripture References (AMP)

Proverbs 31:10   Proverbs 31:28-31

Proverbs 31:25,26

---

* *Life Application Bible,* New International Version edition (Wheaton, IL: Tyndale House Publishers, 1988, 1989, 1990, 1991), commentary at bottom of p. 1131.

IV.

Grandparent's Prayer of Blessing for Children and Grandchildren

Dear Grandparent:

The [Hebrew] father's place in the [traditional Jewish] home is fittingly shown by the beautiful custom of blessing the children, a custom which dates back to Isaac and Jacob. To this day, in many homes, the father blesses his children on Friday nights, on Rosh Hashanah eve and on Yom Kippur before leaving for the synagogue....

In very ancient times, the father or patriarch was the ruler of home and family. He made laws and enforced them. Later, however, laws were instituted by teachers, parents, judges, and kings. The father, as the master of the house, was looked up to for support and depended on for guidance.*

Jacob blessed his children and two of his grandchildren. I encourage you to pray the following prayer, which is based on a translation of the traditional Hebrew father's blessing upon his children.

Prayer

Father, I receive, welcome, and acknowledge each of my children and grandchildren as a delightful blessing from You. I speak Your blessings upon them and over them.

Grandchildren, I bless you in the name of Jesus, proclaiming the blessings of God, my Redeemer, upon you. May He give you wisdom, a reverential fear of God, and a heart of love.

May He create in you the desire to attend to His words, a willing and obedient heart that you may consent and submit to His sayings and walk in His ways. May your eyes look straight ahead with purpose for the future. May your tongue be as the pen of a ready writer, writing mercy and kindness upon the tablets of your heart. May you speak the truth in love. May your hands do the works of the Father; may your feet walk the paths which He has foreordained for you.

I have no greater joy than this: to hear that my children and grandchildren are living their lives in the truth.

May the Lord prepare you and your future mate to love and honor one another, and may He grant to your union upright sons and daughters who will live in accordance with His Word. May your source of livelihood be honorable and secure, so that you will earn a living with your own hands. May you always worship God in spirit and in truth.

I pray above all things that you may always prosper and be in health, even as your soul prospers. "I know the thoughts and plans that I have for you, says the Lord, thoughts and plans for welfare and peace and not for evil, to give you hope in your final outcome" (Jer. 29:11 AMP).

In the name of Jesus I pray. Amen.

Scripture References

Psalm 127:3 AMP	Ephesians 2:10 AMP
Philippians 2:13 AMP	3 John 4 AMP
Proverbs 4:20	1 Thessalonians 4:11,12 NIV
Psalm 45:1	John 4:23
Proverbs 3:3 AMP	3 John 2
Ephesians 4:15	

---

* Ben M. Edidin, *Jewish Customs and Ceremonies* (New York: Hebrew Publishing Company, 1941), p. 23.

Peace in the Family

Father, in the name of Jesus, I come before You on behalf of our children and their children. I thank You for pouring Your Spirit upon each family from on high. By Your grace and power their wilderness has become a fruitful field, and they value their fruitful field as a forest. I believe in my heart and say that justice dwells in their wilderness, and righteousness [religious and moral rectitude in every area and relation] abides in their fruitful field. The effect of righteousness will be peace [internal and external], and the result of righteousness will be quietness and confident trust forever.

In the name of Jesus I bind my children and their children to truth, mercy, and grace. As they grow in grace and in the knowledge of Jesus Christ each family will dwell in a peaceable habitation, in safe dwellings, and in quiet resting places. Father, I ask You to give them stability in their times, abundance of salvation, wisdom, and knowledge. There, reverent fear and worship of the Lord are their treasure and Yours.

O Lord, be gracious to each family; we have waited [expectantly] for You. Be the Arm of Your servants—their strength and defense—every morning, their salvation in the time of trouble.

Father, we thank You for their peace, their safety, and their welfare this day. Hallelujah! Amen.

Scripture References (AMP)

Isaiah 32:15-18   Isaiah 33:2,6

Hedge of Protection

Father, in the name of Jesus, I lift up to You my grandchildren who are at home and away from home and pray a hedge of protection around them. Taking my place in intercession I stand in the gap before You on their behalf. I thank You, Father, that You are a wall of fire round about them and that You set Your angels round about them.

I thank You, Father, that my grandchildren dwell in the secret place of the Most High and abide under the shadow of the Almighty. I say of You, Lord, You are their refuge and fortress; in You will they trust. You cover these precious grandchildren with Your feathers, and under Your wings they trust. In the name of Jesus I set them free from fear and they shall not be afraid of the terror by night or the arrow that flies by day. Only with their eyes will they behold and see the reward of the wicked.

You are my Lord, and I declare and decree that You are a refuge and fortress to my grandchildren; no evil shall befall them—no accident will overtake them— neither shall any plague or calamity come near them. For You give Your angels charge over them to keep them in all Your ways.

Father, because You have set Your love upon my grandchildren You will deliver them. They shall call upon

You, and You will answer them. You will be with them in trouble and will satisfy them with long life and show them Your salvation. Not a hair of their heads shall perish. Amen.

Scripture References

Ezekiel 22:30	Psalm 91:4,5 AMP
Zechariah 2:5	Psalm 91:8-11 AMP
Psalm 34:7	Psalm 91:14-16 AMP
Psalm 91:1,2 AMP	Luke 21:18

Grandchildren at School

Father, in Jesus' name, I affirm Your Word this day over my grandchildren as they pursue their education and training at school. You are effectually at work in them, creating within them the power and desire to please You. They are the head and not the tail, above and not beneath.

You will cause my grandchildren to find favor, good understanding, and high esteem in the sight of God, their teachers, and classmates. I ask You to give them wisdom and understanding as knowledge is presented to them in all fields of study and endeavor.

Father, thank You for giving _____ (name your grandchildren) an appreciation for education, and for helping them to understand that the source and beginning of all knowledge is in You. You are creating in them the appetite of the diligent, and they are abundantly supplied with educational resources; their thoughts are those of the steadily diligent, which tend only to achievement.

Thank You that they are growing in wisdom and knowledge. I will not cease to pray for my grandchildren, asking that they be filled with the knowledge of Your will, bearing fruit in every good work.

Father, I thank You that my grandchildren have divine protection because they dwell in the secret place of the

Most High. I bind my grandchildren to truth, mercy, and grace, their feet to paths of righteousness; they will trust and find their refuge in You and stand rooted and grounded in Your love. I loose wrong perceptions about who You are, and they shall not be led astray by philosophies of men and teaching that is contrary to truth. You are their shield and buckler, protecting them from attacks or threats.

Thank You for the angels whom You have assigned to them to accompany, defend, and preserve them in all their ways of obedience and service. My grandchildren are growing and becoming established in Your love, which drives all fear out of doors.

I pray that the teachers of my grandchildren will be godly men and women of integrity. Give their teachers understanding hearts and wisdom in order that they may walk in the ways of piety and virtue, revering Your holy name. Amen.

Scripture References

Philippians 2:13	Psalm 91:1,2
Deuteronomy 28:1,2,13	Ephesians 4:14
Proverbs 3:4 AMP	Psalm 91:3-11
1 Kings 4:29	Ephesians 1:17
Daniel 1:4	Psalm 112:8

Proverbs 1:4,7   Ephesians 3:17

Proverbs 3:13   Matthew 18:18

Proverbs 4:5   James 1:5

Colossians 1:9,10

School Systems and Grandchildren

Father, we thank You that the entrance of Your Word brings light and that You watch over Your Word to perform it. We bring before You the _____ (name them) school system(s) and the men and women who are in positions of authority within the school system(s).

We pray that men and women of integrity—blameless and complete in Your sight—remain in these positions, but that the wicked be cut off and the treacherous be rooted out, in the name of Jesus. Father, we thank You for God-fearing people in these positions, and we pray that You will protect them in all their ways of service and obedience.

Father, we bring our grandchildren before You. Speaking Your Word boldly and confidently, we affirm that we and our households are saved in the name of Jesus. We are redeemed from the curse of the law, for Jesus was made a curse for us. *Our grandsons and granddaughters are not given to another people.* We enjoy our grandchildren, and they shall not go into captivity, in the name of Jesus.

We bind our grandchildren's thought patterns to Your will for their lives and ask You to give them the courage to shrink from whatever might offend You, Father. May they prove themselves to be blameless, guileless, innocent, and uncontaminated children of God, without blemish (fault-less, unrebukable), in the midst of a crooked and wicked generation, holding out to it and offering to all the Word of life. Thank You, Father, for giving them knowledge and skill in all learning and wisdom and for bringing them into favor with those around them.

Father, we enforce the triumphant victory of our Lord Jesus Christ, proclaiming that the mercy and loving-kindness of the Lord are from everlasting to everlasting—and this generation shall arise and shine for their light has come. Thank You for commanding Your ministering spirits to go forth and police the hallways and classrooms and all other areas of school buildings, exposing plots of the evil one.

In the name of Jesus, we bind the minds of the school personnel to the mind of Christ, and bind their plans to Your plans for the education of our grandchildren. We praise You, Father, that we shall see them walking in the ways of piety and virtue, revering Your name. Those who err in spirit will come to understanding, and those who murmur discontentedly will accept instruction in the way and submit to Your will, carrying out Your purposes in their lives; for You, Father, occupy first place in their hearts. We surround _____ (name them) with our faith.

Father, give Your people boldness to stand up against the forces of darkness that would take away freedom of speech from God-fearing educators in this nation. Thank You, Father, that You are the delivering God. Thank You for intercessors and for those laborers of the harvest who will take a stand for truth and righteousness in Jesus' name. Praise the Lord! Amen.

Scripture References

Psalm 119:130	2 Timothy 2:21 AMP
Jeremiah 1:12	2 Corinthians 7:1 AMP
Proverbs 2:10-12 AMP	1 Corinthians 6:18 AMP
Proverbs 2:21,22 AMP	Romans 13:13 AMP
Acts 16:31	Ephesians 5:4
Galatians 3:13	2 Timothy 2:22
Deuteronomy 28:32,41	Matthew 18:18
Proverbs 22:6 AMP	2 Timothy 2:26
Philippians 2:15,16 AMP	Hebrews 1:14
Daniel 1:17 AMP	Colossians 2:3 AMP
Daniel 1:9	Isaiah 29:23,24 AMP
1 John 2:16,17 AMP	

For Your Grandchildren's Future

Father, Your Word declares that children's children are the crown of the aged. I pray to You today, declaring that my grandchildren are being raised as You desire and they will follow the path You choose. Father, I pray Your Word this day over _____ (name your grandchildren). I thank You that Your Word goes out and will not return unto You void, but will accomplish what it says it will do.

Thank You for creating in my grandchildren a willing and obedient spirit and attitude. They are godly children who are not ashamed or afraid to honor You and their parents. They stand convinced that You are the Almighty God. I am thankful that as they mature, they will remember You and not pass by the opportunity of a relationship with Your Son, Jesus. Your great blessings will be upon our grandchildren because they are keeping Your ways. I thank You for Your blessings heaped upon them and for drawing them to a life of obedience by Your goodness.

Heavenly Father, I thank You now that laborers will be sent into the paths of our grandchildren, preparing the way for their salvation through Your Son, Jesus. I am thankful that You are keeping their feet from the traps of the devil and that they will be delivered to salvation through the purity of Your Son. You have given my grandchildren the grace and strength to walk the narrow pathway to Your kingdom.

I pray that, just as Jesus increased in wisdom and stature, You bless these children with the same wisdom and pour out Your favor and wisdom openly to them.

I praise You in advance for the spouse You have for each of my grandchildren. Father, Your Word declares that You desire for children to be pure and honorable, waiting for marriage. I speak blessings to each future union and believe that each husband and wife will be well suited to each other and each household will be in godly order, holding fast to the love of Jesus Christ. Continue to prepare my grandchildren to be the men and women of God that You desire each of them to be.

I believe that my grandchildren shall be diligent and hard-working, never lazy or undisciplined. Your Word promises great blessing to their houses, and they shall always be satisfied and will always increase. Godliness is profitable unto their houses, and they shall receive the promise of life and all that is to come.

Father, thank You for protecting and guiding my grandchildren.

In Jesus' name I pray. Amen.

Scripture References

Psalm 127:3

Isaiah 54:13

Isaiah 55:11

Proverbs 22:6

1 Peter 5:7

Ephesians 6:4

Deuteronomy 6:7

2 Corinthians 12:9

Ephesians 6:1-3

2 Timothy 1:12

Proverbs 8:17,32

Luke 19:10

Matthew 9:38

2 Corinthians 2:11

2 Timothy 2:26

Job 22:30

Matthew 7:14

Luke 2:52

Hebrews 13:4

1 Thessalonians 4:3

Ephesians 5:22-25

2 Timothy 1:13

Proverbs 13:11

Proverbs 20:13

Romans 12:11

1 Timothy 4:8

1 John 3:8

John 10:10

Matthew 18:18

John 14:13

Psalm 91:1,11

Your Grandchildren's Relationships

Father, I pray that my grandchildren will have healthy relationships in all walks of life. May they love You because You first loved them. Help us to be good examples, teaching them to love You with all their intellect, strength, and might so they will keep Your laws and obey Your commands. I bind mercy and truth on the tablets of their hearts and minds so that they will remember to be truthful and kind from deep within their hearts; then they will find favor with both You and man. I pray that they will acquire a reputation for good judgment and common sense.

Father, we will demonstrate good manners, teaching our grandchildren to be considerate and respectful of others. They will esteem others and encourage them with words of love and grace. In the name of Jesus, You are making Your face to shine upon and enlighten my grandchildren. They will grow up and be imitators of You, gracious (kind, merciful, and giving favor) to others because they have received favor from You. They are the head and not the tail, above only and not beneath.

Thank You for giving them a heart and mind to seek first Your kingdom and Your righteousness. When they diligently seek good, they produce favor. They are a blessing to You, Lord, and a blessing to _____ (name them: family members, neighbors, school mates, friends, teachers, etc.). Grace (favor) is with them because they love the Lord Jesus in sincerity. Thank You for extending favor, honor, and love to them so that they are always flowing in Your love, Father. You are pouring out upon them the Spirit of favor. You crown them with glory and honor, for they are Your children—Your workmanship.

In the name of Jesus, I declare that my grandchildren are a success today. Each of them is someone very special to You, Lord, and is growing in You—waxing strong in spirit. Father, thank You for giving them knowledge and skill in all learning and wisdom. You are bringing them to find favor, compassion, and loving-kindness with everyone. They are obtaining favor in the sight of all who look upon them this day, in the name of Jesus. They are filled with Your fullness—rooted and grounded in love. You are doing exceeding abundantly above all that they ask or think, for Your mighty power is taking over in them.

Thank You, Father, that my grandchildren are well-favored by You and by man.

In Jesus' name I pray. Amen.

Scripture References

Luke 2:52 AMP

Proverbs 3:1-4 TLB

Numbers 6:25 AMP

Deuteronomy 28:13 AMP

Matthew 6:33 AMP

Proverbs 11:27 AMP

Ephesians 6:24 AMP

Esther 2:15,17

Psalm 118:25 AMP

Zechariah 2:8 NLT

Zechariah 12:10 AMP

Psalm 8:5 AMP

Ephesians 2:10 AMP

Luke 2:40

Daniel 1:17,9 AMP

Ephesians 3:19,20

Favor for Grandchildren

Father, I pray that my grandchildren, _____ (name them), will invite Jesus into their hearts at an early age and develop a personal relationship with You. You make Your face to shine upon them and enlighten them. You are gracious (kind, merciful, and giving favor) to them. They are the head and not the tail, above only and not beneath.

Thank You that they are increasing in favor with You by seeking Your kingdom and Your righteousness and diligently seeking good. My grandchildren are a blessing to You, Lord, and a blessing to _____ (name them: family, neighbors, school mates, business associates, etc.). Grace (favor) is with them because they love the Lord Jesus in sincerity. Because they are Your beloved children, You extend favor, honor, and love to them, so that they are always flowing in Your love, Father. You are pouring out upon my grandchildren the spirit of favor and crowning them with glory and honor. They are Your workmanship.

My heart overflows with praise and thanksgiving because of who You are, my Father. Thank You for giving my grandchildren the power and ability to succeed. You call each one by name, and they are very special to You.

They are growing in You—waxing strong in spirit—because You, Father, are giving them knowledge and skill in all learning and wisdom.

Thank You that my grandchildren are increasing in favor, compassion, and loving-kindness with others by respecting authority. They cheer others on, encouraging them in their pursuits. They obtain favor in the sight of all who look upon them this day, in the name of Jesus. They are filled with Your fullness—rooted and grounded in love.

You are doing exceeding abundantly above all that I ask or think, according to the power that is at work in me. These grandchildren were chosen by You before the foundation of the world, and I will encourage them as they fulfill the destiny You have planned for them.

Thank You, Father, that my grandchildren are well-favored by You and by man, and they are a blessing to everyone they meet, in Jesus' name! Amen.

Scripture References

Numbers 6:25 AMP	Psalm 8:5
Deuteronomy 28:13	Ephesians 2:10
Matthew 6:33	Luke 2:40
Proverbs 11:27	Daniel 1:17
Ephesians 6:24	Daniel 1:9 AMP

Luke 6:38   Esther 2:15

Zechariah 12:10 AMP   Ephesians 3:17,19,20

Luke 2:52

For Your Grandchildren To Fulfill Their Divine Destiny

Father, as I encourage my grandchildren according to Your ways, I believe that they will dedicate themselves to live for You. They won't know everything the future holds for them, but they will know that Your plans are to prosper them and not to harm them, that You plan to give them hope and a future. They will trust You to lead them and to be their guide in life. Lord, I trust You to prepare my grandchildren now for Your life plan for them. Thank You that they will have the wisdom to discern the right timing for what You would have them do in each season of their lives. Each one will choose to love, obey, and cleave unto You with his/her whole body, soul, and spirit.

Prince of Peace, I ask You to order their steps in Your Word. If college is in his/her future, please help him/her to select the right one. Thank You for providing the means for each one of them to go. Prepare each one for the vocation You have for them. Help them to recognize the skills You have given them so that they can develop them and give the glory to You. Give them understanding and light so that they are quick to learn. Thank You for the wisdom and light that come from You and Your Word.

I believe that my grandchildren depend on You to be a help to them in everything they do. If it is Your will for any or all of them to marry someday, thank You that You are not only preparing each one but also his/her future spouse. Until that time comes, help them to be content.

I declare that my grandchildren depend upon You to provide for them—to supply all the money they need to do Your will. They believe You to instruct and teach them which way to go. They trust that You won't make things confusing for them, but that You make a clear path for them when they put You first.

Thank You that my grandchildren read and meditate on Your words, which are a light for their path. Thank You for Your Holy Spirit, who will reveal to them Your plan for them. I believe my grandchildren treasure life with and for You. Thank You, Father, for holding my grandchildren's futures in the palm of Your hand.

In Jesus' name I pray. Amen.

Scripture References

Jeremiah 29:11

Proverbs 22:6

Proverbs 3:5,6

Psalm 32:8

Psalm 25:5

1 Corinthians 2:9,10

John 16:13

Ephesians 2:10

Deuteronomy 30:20

Ephesians 1:16-18

Proverbs 4:18

Jeremiah 33:3

Romans 8:14

Psalm 119:105

Isaiah 49:16

1 Peter 5:7

Ecclesiastes 3:1-8

Hebrews 13:5

Philippians 4:11,13,19

Wisdom for Your Grandchildren in Daily Living

Praise the Lord! I worship You in spirit and truth. I am blessed, happy, and fortunate, and my offspring shall be mighty upon the earth; this generation of the upright shall be blessed. Heavenly Father, I bind my grandchildren to the clear knowledge of Your will in all wisdom and understanding. I know that Your will and Your Word agree. I bind their desires to Yours so they can know Your plans and purposes for this season in their lives. I pray that they will live in a way that is worthy of You and fully pleasing to You. I believe You will cause their thoughts to agree with Your will so that they may be fruitful in every good work.

Your wisdom is pure and full of compassion. Thank You that my grandchildren are developing in love and are strong in faith, knowing that Your words contain a wealth of wisdom. Whatever situations they may face in life, I thank You that they will always have Your wisdom to do and say the right thing. Teach them the way that You want them to go. Thank You for counseling them and watching carefully over them. Thank You for the Holy Spirit; He is their teacher, helper, and guide, and I believe He is active in their lives.

My grandchildren will not be afraid or confused, because Your Word brings them light and understanding. Although there are many voices in the world, they will follow the voice of the Good Shepherd, who laid down His life for the sheep.

Thank You for the wise parents, teachers, caregivers, friends, and pastors You have placed in my grandchildren's lives to teach and instruct them. I pray that my grandchildren will seek godly counsel from them. When they need to make an important decision, I pray that they will follow the peace that comes from knowing Your Word.

As much as is possible for me to do, I dedicate my grandchildren to You, and believe that their plans will succeed. I trust You with their lives and everything in them. I thank You for Your wisdom that causes them to stand and to walk wisely, making the most of their time.

In Jesus' name I pray. Amen.

Scripture References

Colossians 1:9 NIV

1 John 5:14,15 AMP

Joshua 1:8

Colossians 3:16

Colossians 1:10 AMP

Proverbs 16:3 AMP

Psalm 16:7 AMP

John 14:26 AMP

1 Corinthians 14:33

Proverbs 6:20-23

John 10:1-5,15

Proverbs 2:6 AMP

Colossian 1:10

James 3:17 AMP

Philippians 1:9 AMP

Romans 4:20

James 1:5,6 AMP

Psalm 32:8 NIV

Proverbs 16:3 NIV

Psalm 118:8 AMP

Hebrews 12:14

Psalm 119:99,130,133

Proverbs 19:21

Ephesians 5:15,16 NAS

For Your Grandchildren's Wise Choice of Friends

Father, I come boldly to Your throne of grace to ask You to help my grandchildren meet some new friends. I know that You are the source of love and friendship, but that You also desire to express Your love and friendship toward my grandchildren through others. I am convinced that it is Your will for my grandchildren to have godly friendships with members of both sexes.

Your Word reveals the purpose and value of healthy friendships. It is not the quantity but the quality of friends that matters. Holy Spirit, teach my grandchildren what they need to know to be quality friends. Help them to show themselves friendly to others and to love their friends at all times. In the name of Jesus, I believe that because they have been taught truth they will purpose to live in peace as much as is possible. I pray that they and their friends will encourage each other. Help them to rid themselves of any prejudice or partiality. I pray that they will not [attempt to] hold [and] practice the faith of our Lord Jesus Christ, [the Lord] of glory [together with snobbery]! Instead, they will welcome and receive others as You, Father, have received them.

Help them to be kind, humble, and gentle, and to forgive those who need forgiveness, because they are forgiven.

I pray that they and their new friends will be in perfect harmony and full agreement, and that there will be no dissention, factionalism, or division among them, but that they will be perfectly united. Help them to stand firm in a united spirit and to be of a single mind, one in purpose and intention, their hearts knit together in love. May their love for one another be so strong that, as the Lord Jesus did, they would be willing to lay down their very lives for one another.

For my grandchildren's new friends, I thank You.

In Jesus' name I pray. Amen.

Scripture References

Hebrews 4:16	James 2:1 AMP
James 1:17	Romans 15:7 AMP
Psalm 84:11	Ephesians 4:2,32 AMP
Ecclesiastes 4:9,10	1 Corinthians 1:10 AMP
Proverbs 13:20	Philippians 1:27 AMP
Proverbs 18:24	Philippians 2:2 AMP
Proverbs 17:17	Colossians 2:2
Romans 12:18	John 15:13

For Your Grandchildren To Positively Affect Their Peers

by Kathy Witherell
Member of the Word Ministries Prayer Team

Thank You, God, for the fertile, rich soil of my grand-children's hearts. What a beautiful place for me to plant seeds from the Word of God that will blossom! Like sunflowers that turn their petals toward the sun and follow it all the day long, let my grandchildren turn their hearts toward Your Son. I love teaching them when they sit in my house. Teach them to number their days that they may gain a heart of wisdom. Lead them on paths of righteous-ness for Your name's sake.

Lord, I pray that You strategically place them among godly friends who keep Your ways. You promise to give long life to those who honor their father and mother. Guard their hearts and minds from the influence of the world and the pressure to give in to temptation. Teach them to consider their steps and choose wisely according to Your Word. Lord, I know they will reap blessings from obedience to godly authority in their lives.

Praise You that my children and grandchildren are Your sons and daughters. Bless them as they grow in the knowledge that their bodies are temples of the Holy

Spirit, that there is great virtue in keeping themselves pure in body, soul, and spirit. When they are tempted to succumb to peer pressure, remind them of the loyalty and devotion of their friend Jesus.

How blessed are they that the Father chose them in Christ before the foundations of the world, that they should be holy and without blame before Him in love. We place the armor of God upon our grandchildren, knowing that the living Word of God will help them be victorious during times of trouble.

Thank You that they are Your workmanship created in Christ Jesus for good works, that they should walk in them. Let me have mercy when they make mistakes. I declare that they will influence, they will lead, and they will draw others to You as the light of Jesus is reflected in them. Their light will not be hidden, but it will shine before men, that they may see their good works.

I thank You that from childhood they have known the Holy Scriptures, which are able to make them wise for salvation. I declare, Lord, that their times are in Your hands and that You shall hide them in the secret place of Your presence. I praise You for my grandchildren, who will declare, "I have kept the ways of the Lord and have not wickedly departed from God."

Scripture References (NKJV)

Psalm 90:12

Psalm 23:3

Psalm 18:21

Psalm 31:14,15

Psalm 31:20

Matthew 5:15

Ephesians 2:10

2 Timothy 3:15

Ephesians 6:2,3

Dealing With a Grandchild With *ADD/ADHD*

Dear Grandparent:

In these last days, Satan is working harder than ever to destroy our children. One of the areas of his attack is what psychologists and educators call Attention Deficit Disorder (ADD)/Attention Deficit Hyperactivity Disorder (ADHD). These disorders are tools of the enemy to disrupt households, causing confusion, frustration, division, and every evil work. Their effects are far reaching.

Working with children with ADD/ADHD can be frustrating and discouraging, but as believers we know that God's Word, prayer, understanding caretakers, Christian counseling, medication (if necessary), and peers can help them become overcomers. You may desire to form or join a support/prayer group of grandparents who have grandchildren with this disorder.

In our ministry to these special children, we must remember that, according to 2 Corinthians 10:4, "the weapons of our warfare are not carnal, but mighty through God to the pulling down of strong holds." Psalm 107:20 AMP says of the Lord's intervention on behalf of those in need, "He sends forth His word and heals them and rescues them from the pit and destruction." Prayer, according to the Word of God, will avail much. (James 5:16.)

Declare and decree victory for the child as you teach and direct him/her through the following prayers.

The first two prayers were written by a grandmother, one of our former associates at Word Ministries, whose grandson was diagnosed with ADD/ADHD. When he lived with them, they prayed together each morning before he left for school.

The third prayer and the following series of daily prayers were based on conversations and prayer times that I had with this young man. He and I cried and laughed together in my office, where we talked privately and confidentially.

At times, he would ask to sit in a class where I was teaching, and later we discussed the subject matter. For instance, we talked about abandonment issues and how Jesus felt when He was on the cross. He was never shy about asking for prayer when he was having a problem. He was thrilled when he learned that I was sharing these prayers with others. Even though he has moved on, I believe that these prayers are printed on the tablets of his heart and mind. I pray that the Holy Spirit will cause the Word of God to rise up on the inside of this young man when he most needs it.

When you pray these prayers with your grandchild, I encourage you to explain in simple language the meaning of the terms found in them. Remember, the child's imagination is creating pictures with the words he/she hears and speaks.

Do not overburden the child with the following prayers but lead him/her gently, keeping in mind his/her age and attention span. Do not demand that the child pray an entire prayer at one sitting. The Holy Spirit will be your guide. As the child prays, listen carefully, allowing the child to express his/her feelings, fears, thoughts, and ideas. Ask the Holy Spirit for discernment; it can be difficult to separate seriousness from horseplay. If you give the child time, he/she will let you know the difference.

Grandpartents can bridge the generational gap by listening with an understanding ear and offering encouragement and prayers filled with unconditional love. Assure your grandchild of your belief in God's love and understanding for him/her. "For I know the plans I have for you, says the Lord." God's plans for your grandchild "are plans for good and not for evil, to give you a future and a hope. In those days when you pray, I will listen" (Jer. 29:11,12 TLB).

Prayers To Be Prayed by the Child

I.

Coming Against ADD/ADHD

Father, in the name of Jesus, I bind my mind to the mind of Christ and loose myself from word curses spoken about me, to me, and by me. I loose ADD/ADHD and its effects from my mind and emotions. I say that I have the mind of Christ (the Messiah) and hold the thoughts (feelings and purposes) of His heart; I am able to concentrate and stay focused on each task.

I am a disciple (taught by You, Lord, and obedient to Your will), and great is my peace and undisturbed composure. Father, You have not given me a spirit of fear, but [You have given me a spirit] of power and of love and of a calm, well-balanced mind and discipline and self-control. In the name of Jesus, I bind my emotions to the control of the Holy Spirit.

In the name of Jesus, I loose rebellious thoughts, defiant behavior, tantrums, and hyperactivity from myself. Help me speak peace and love to the situations in which I find myself. I cast down imaginations and every high thing that would exalt itself against the knowledge of You, Lord, and bring into captivity every thought to the obedience of Christ.

Father, I ask for Your wisdom to reside in me each day as I learn new techniques for handling stressful incidents.

Father, Your Word says not to worry about anything but to pray and ask You for everything I need and to give thanks when I pray, and Your peace will keep my heart and mind in Christ Jesus. The peace You give me is so great that I cannot understand it.

Thank You for keeping my mind quiet and at peace. I declare that I am an overcomer. I bind my emotions to the control of the Holy Spirit. ADD/ADHD will no longer control me; the Holy Spirit is helping me take charge of my behavior.

In the name of Jesus I pray. Amen.

Scripture References

1 Corinthians 2:16 AMP

Isaiah 54:13 AMP

2 Timothy 1:7 AMP

2 Corinthians 10:5

Philippians 4:6,7 ICB

Isaiah 26:3

Revelation 12:11

II.

Making New Friends

Father, I am asking You to supply me with good friends I can relate to, spend time with, and enjoy as You intended. I desire to develop relationships that will be lasting and helpful to both me and my friends.

Father, thank You for giving me a sound mind so I can be self-restrained. I am alert—and above all things, I purpose to have intense and unfailing love for You and for others, for I know love covers a multitude of sins [forgives and disregards the offenses of others].

I bind my behavior and attitude to the fruit of the Spirit so others will want to be around me. I purpose to bridle my tongue and speak words of kindness. I will not insist on having my own way, and I will not act unbecomingly. When someone is unkind and falsely accuses me, help me to maintain a cool spirit and be slow to anger. I commit to plant seeds of love, and I thank You for preparing hearts ahead of time to receive me as a friend and as a blessing to their lives.

Father, thank You for causing me to find favor, compassion, and loving-kindness with others.

Thank You, Lord, for my new friends.

In Jesus' name, amen.

Scripture References

1 Peter 4:7,8 AMP

Proverbs 21:23

1 Corinthians 13:4,5

Proverbs 18:24 AMP

James 1:19 AMP

1 Corinthians 3:6

Daniel 1:9 AMP

III.

Having a Bad Day

Father, this was not a good day. My scores were low. It was a hard day for me at school and at home. I feel that I messed up a lot. Because I know that You love me unconditionally and You are not holding anything against me, I come to talk with You.

Father, You expect me to be accountable to You, my teachers, and my parents for my behavior.* I ask Your forgiveness for acting mean and disrespectful to _____. I acknowledge my misbehavior, and I ask You to forgive me for _____.

Thank You, Lord, for helping me as I learn good social skills and how to do unto others as I want them to do unto me.

Father, I release my disappointment to You, and I believe that tomorrow will be a great day! I look forward to the new day with its new beginnings.

In the name of Jesus I pray. Amen.

Scripture References

Romans 8:33-39 NIV	Matthew 15:4 NIV
2 Corinthians 5:18 TLB	1 John 1:9 TLB
Matthew 12:36 NIV	Luke 6:31 NIV
Romans 13:1-5 NIV	Proverbs 4:18

---

* NOTE TO PARENT: Effective reprimands should be brief and directed at the child's behavior, not at the character of the child. Help the child assume responsibility for his/her actions, and to acknowledge and ask forgiveness when appropriate.

IV.

Living Each Day

Monday:

Father, in the name of Jesus, I thank You for giving me life. You picked me out for Your very own even before the foundation of the world—before I was ever born. You saw me while I was being formed in my mother's womb, and You know all about ADD/ADHD.

Lord, You see the weird things I do, and You know all my weird thoughts even before I think them. In the name of Jesus I bind my thoughts to goodness and mercy, and loose bad thoughts and feelings toward others and myself from my thought patterns.

Help my parents, teachers, and especially the bus driver to help me do right things. Help me to be kind to others.

In the name of Jesus I pray. Amen.

Scripture References

Ephesians 1:4 AMP

Psalm 139:2 TLB

Psalm 139:13-16 TLB

Ephesians 4:32 TLB

Tuesday:

Father, Psalm 91 says that You have assigned angels to me—giving them [special] charge over me to accompany and defend and preserve me in all my ways.

Lord, I need Your help. Sometimes my weird thoughts scare me, and I don't like the way I behave. I become so frightened and confused that I have to do something: run, make noises—even scream or try to hurt someone. These actions separate me from playmates; and when they don't want to be my friends, I am hurt and disappointed and angry.

I am asking You, Father, to help me form new behavior patterns and successfully overcome the disobedience and defiance that cause my parents and teachers anguish. I don't like to see them all upset, even though I laugh about it sometimes.

Thank You for helping me overcome obsessive-compulsive actions that create confusion for me and others around me. Even when others don't want me around, You will never abandon me. You will always be with me to help me and give me support.

In the name of Jesus I pray. Amen.

Scripture References

Psalm 91:11 AMP	Psalm 27:10 TLB
Romans 7:21-25 TLB	Hebrews 13:5 AMP

Wednesday:

Father, thank You for my parents, grandparents, wise counselors, and teachers who understand me and are helping me learn good behavior patterns. Help me to listen and develop good relationships with others—especially other children.

Thank You for giving me the ability to learn how to express my anger appropriately; I rejoice every time I have a victory. Your Son, Jesus, said that He has given me power to overcome all the obstacles that ADD/ADHD causes in my life.

In His name I pray. Amen.

Scripture References

Ephesians 4:26 TLB   Luke 10:19 NIV

Thursday:

Father, I believe in my heart that Your Son, Jesus, is my Lord and Master and that He has come to live in my heart. Thank You for giving me the mind of Christ (the Messiah), His thoughts (feelings and purposes).

Lord, You are with me when my thoughts get jumbled up, and You have sent the Holy Spirit to help me concentrate and stay focused on each task at home and at school. I am a disciple [taught by You, Lord, and obedient to Your will], and great is my peace and undisturbed composure. Thank You for giving me Your helmet of salvation to protect my thought life.

In the name of Jesus I pray. Amen.

Scripture References

Romans 10:9,10 NIV   Isaiah 54:13 AMP
1 Corinthians 2:16 AMP   1 Thessalonians 5:8 NIV
John 16:13 NIV

Friday:

Father, You have not given me a spirit of fear, but You have given me a spirit of power and of love and of a calm, well-balanced mind and discipline and self-control. Thank You that as I grow in the grace and knowledge of Jesus Christ, You are creating in me a willing heart to be obedient.

Forgive me for throwing tantrums, and help me recognize and use Your power that is working in me to loose, crush, smash, and annihilate the destructive ideas that cause them. The Holy Spirit is my helper. Thank You for giving me the ability to channel hyperactivity in constructive, productive ways.

I choose to speak peace and love into the situations that confront me and make me feel uncomfortable and out of control.

In the name of Jesus I pray. Amen.

Scripture References

2 Timothy 1:7 AMP   Philippians 2:13

2 Peter 3:18   John 14:16 AMP

Exodus 35:5

Saturday:

Father, sometimes awful thoughts come to me, and I command the voices that tell me bad things to be quiet and leave me in the name of Jesus.

Lord, in Your Word You said that I can make choices. I choose to cast down imaginations that cause me to feel afraid and angry; these thoughts are not Your thoughts. You love me, and I bind my thought patterns to the good things You have provided for me.

Father, I ask for Your wisdom to reside in me each day as I learn new techniques for handling stressful incidents.

In the name of Jesus I pray. Amen.

Scripture References

Deuteronomy 30:19,20 TLB   Isaiah 55:8 TLB

2 Corinthians 10:5   Philippians 4:8 TLB

Sunday:

Father, there are so many everyday things that worry and torment me. I feel so different from other people.

Lord, Your Word says not to worry about anything but to pray and ask You for everything I need and to give thanks when I pray, and Your peace will keep my heart and mind in Christ Jesus. The peace You give me is so great that I cannot understand it.

When I resist the temptation to be anxious, You keep my mind quiet and at peace. I declare that I am an overcomer, and by submitting to Your control I am learning self-control.

Father, I thank You for teaching me how to be a good friend to those You are sending to be my friends.

In the name of Jesus I pray. Amen.

Scripture References

Philippians 4:6,7 ICB   Revelation 12:11

Isaiah 26:3 AMP   Galatians 5:23 AMP

*Prayer To Be Prayed
by the Grandparent*

Dear Grandparent,

Much prayer and faith are required to see the ADD/ADHD grandchild as God sees him/her. When emotions erupt, the challenges become great and you may feel overwhelmed.

You will need mega doses of godly wisdom, spiritual discernment, and mental and emotional alertness to overcome those times of weariness, bewilderment, and anxiety. Your words are powerful! They will give your grandchild comfort and hope—or they can reinforce the child's belief that he/she is bad and that something terrible is wrong with him/her. Do not speak unadvisedly; your words can heal, or wound.

As the occasion arises teach your grandchild to pray, and reinforce his/her prayers with unconditional love. Often your image of another individual—even your grandchild—can only be changed as you pray according to God's will and purpose for him/her. I wrote the following personal prayer for my friend and associate and her husband who were raising their ADD/ADHD grandson. I witnessed the heartache, delight, exasperation—the full gamut of emotions involved in this challenging experience. But through it all, God was faithful!

Prayer

Father, in the name of Jesus, I thank You for this very special grandchild. You see my confusion, anxiety, frustration, and bewilderment as I attempt to rear him [tenderly] in the training, discipline, counsel, and admonition of the Lord. Forgive me for times when I knowingly or unknowingly irritate and provoke him/her to anger [exasperate him/her to resentment].

You see my intense pain when I observe the rejection my grandchild suffers. By faith I forgive adults who speak harsh words against him/her and our family. In the name of Jesus I loose from our family all word curses spoken to us, about us, or by us. Children refuse to play with him/her and it hurts, even though I understand. I know that those who have never walked in our shoes cannot fully understand us.

But, Lord, where others are unmerciful and unkind, You are merciful and kind. Surely, goodness and mercy shall follow us all the days of our lives, and we shall dwell in Your house forever. Hide us in the secret place of Your presence, and keep us secretly in Your pavilion from the strife of tongues.

Lord, perfect the fruit of my lips, that I may offer to You effective praise and thanksgiving for this grandchild who is a blessing from You. His/Her intellect astounds me, and his/her wit is a delight. I ask You for divine intervention and guidance as I parent him/her according to the way that he/she should go. I thank You for the awesomeness of Your handiwork and the techniques that You have given him/her to survive—to overcome emotional turmoil—and the ability to function in this world around us. Truly, this grandchild is fearfully and wonderfully made. I plead the blood of Jesus over him/her to protect him/her in every situation.

You have a divine purpose for this special grandchild.
You have foreordained steps that he/she is to walk in,
works that he/she is to do. Help me to look at his/her
strengths and weaknesses realistically, that I may know
how to help him/her develop and demonstrate self-control
techniques. Forgive me for times when I lose patience and
berate him/her for his/her behavior. Sometimes, I lose
sight of who he/she really is. Anoint my eyes to see
him/her as You see him/her.

Father, help me to speak words of grace; anoint my
lips to speak excellent and princely things over, about, and
to him/her. May the opening of my lips be for right
things. Help me to give him/her healthy doses of unconditional love, administer to him/her appropriate discipline
for misbehavior, and reward him/her for good behavior.
Anoint my lips with coals of fire from Your altar, that I
may speak words that comfort, encourage, strengthen, and
honor him/her. Keep watch at the door of my lips, and
forgive me when my patience has come to an end.

Father, You are my comforter, counselor, helper, intercessor, advocate, strengthener, and standby. Whatever
comes my way, help me to consider it wholly joyful,
allowing endurance and steadfastness and patience to have
full play and do a thorough work, so that I may be
perfectly and fully developed [with no defects], lacking in
nothing. When I am deficient in wisdom, I will ask of

You, and You will give wisdom to me liberally and ungrudgingly, without reproaching or finding fault in me.

I pray that I may be invigorated and strengthened with all power according to the might of Your glory, [to exercise] every kind of endurance and patience (perseverance and forbearance) with joy.

Father, You have seen the tears in the night season, and I know that I shall experience the joy that comes in the morning times. You are my exceeding joy! You are my wisdom, righteousness, sanctification, and redemption. Thank You for being a constant companion.

Lord, I see my grandchild, _____, growing and becoming strong in spirit, increasing in wisdom (in broad and full understanding), in stature and years, and in favor with You and with man.

In the name of Jesus I pray. Amen.

Scripture References

Ephesians 6:4 AMP	Isaiah 6:6,7
Psalm 117:2	Psalm 141:3 AMP
Psalm 23:6	John 14:16 AMP
Psalm 31:20 AMP	James 1:2,4,5 AMP
Hebrews 13:15	Colossians 1:11 AMP
Psalm 127:3 AMP	Psalm 22:2

Proverbs 22:6	Psalm 30:5
Psalm 139:14	Psalm 43:4
Ephesians 2:10	1 Corinthians 1:30
Proverbs 8:6 AMP	Luke 1:80; 2:52 AMP

Daily Affirmations for Use by the Grandparent

Dear Grandparent,

Often it is very difficult for ADD/ADHD children to learn, to develop new learning techniques in their lives, and to change their negative behavior patterns. When working with them, we need to love them with the God-kind of love and praise them for their accomplishments.

Following are examples of the kinds of positive daily affirmations that can be said to the ADD/ADHD child to help him/her develop a good self-image and to become all that God intends for him/her to be in this life.

Affirmations

• Great job • Well done • I'm very proud of you • Good for you • Neat • Outstanding • That was a smart decision • You are smart • God loves you • I love you • I knew you could do it • I believe in you • I know you are trying • Super-duper • You are a good boy/girl • Way to

go • What an imagination • You are growing up • Good
memory • Amazing • Nice work • What a wise choice •
You are a blessing to me • You are special to me • You are
valuable • You are a gem, a precious jewel • You are more
precious than gold • You are incredible • You are important • Outstanding performance • You are a winner •
Remarkable • Nothing can stop you • Now you've got it •
Excellent • You are catching on • Great • Wonderful •
Good • Terrific • Beautiful • Now you are cooking • You
are fantastic • Beautiful work • Outstanding • You are
spectacular • You are a real trooper • You are unique •
Great discovery • You try so hard • Good try • Good
effort • Magnificent • You've got it • Super work •
Phenomenal • Marvelous • Dynamite • You mean so
much to me • You make me laugh • You brighten my day
• Hurray for you • You are beautiful • You are handsome •
You are a good friend • You are a loving grandson/grand-
daughter • You light up my life • You belong • You are an
important part of our family • We are family • You mean
the world to me • That's right • You are correct • You are a
success • Hurray • You are growing in wisdom every day •
You are a beautiful creation • You are loved • I love you •
wow! • You are a success • You are an overcomer • You are
a grandchild of my love • You are victorious • You are a
ray of sunshine • You are patient • You have a good attitude • You are a doer • You know how to get the job done

• You are a chosen one • You give good hugs • Thank you for being a part of my life • *You are deserving of praise!*

Scripture Passages for Meditation

A GOOD REPORT: Proverbs 15:30; Philippians 4:8

A SOFT ANSWER: Proverbs 15:1

PERFECT LOVE: 1 John 4:18

For Grandchildren With Special Needs

Father and Lord of glory, I come before You boldly
and confidently, knowing that You watch over Your Word
to perform it. You are not a man that You should lie. I
bring before You my grandchild, _____, who is called
physically and/or mentally impaired. Father, my wonderful
Counselor and Prince of Peace, I know that it is Your will
for my grandchild to be made completely whole and
restored in the name of Jesus.

You are the God of miracles; You are love and power
and might. The law of the spirit of life in Christ Jesus has
made us free from the law of sin and death. Throughout
history You have performed miracles, and I am asking
You to perform a miracle in the life of my grandchild.
Lord, You have a purpose and plan for this one who has
special needs, and I ask You to quicken him/her to Your
Word—that he/she may be filled with wisdom and revelation knowledge.

Lord, I loose unbelief and doubt from my heart and
mind in the name of Jesus. I loose all word curses that
have been spoken to, about, or by my grandchild. I
loose blame and condemnation from his/her parents
and grandparents.

Lord, You are the source of every consolation, comfort, and encouragement, and I know that my grandchild is sanctified in spirit, soul, and body.

Almighty God, I pray for a creative miracle for this precious grandchild; for You are the health of his/her countenance and the lifter of his/her head. The joy of the Lord is his/her strength and stronghold! I ask You to commission ministering spirits to go forth as they hearken to Your Word to provide the necessary help for and assistance to _____ (name your grandchild).

In the name of Jesus, I speak life and restoration to damaged brain cells and activation of dormant brain cells. I speak normal intellect for his/her age, and creative miracles to the parts of the body. I bind my grandchild—spirit, soul, and body—to soundness of mind and wholeness.

Nothing is too hard or impossible for You. Because of our faith in You, all things are possible to us who believe. Let my prayers be set forth as incense before You—a sweet fragrance to You! Praise the Lord!

In the name of Jesus I pray. Amen.

Scripture References

Hebrews 4:16 AMP

Jeremiah 1:12 AMP

Ephesians 1:17,18

Psalm 119:89 AMP

Ephesians 2:10 AMP

2 Corinthians 1:3 AMP

1 Thessalonians 5:23 AMP

Psalm 42:11

Psalm 145:14

Psalm 3:3 AMP

Nehemiah 8:10

Psalm 103:20

Luke 1:37 AMP

Mark 9:23 AMP

Psalm 141:2 AMP

Deliverance From Habits

Father, I thank You for my grandchildren, and pray especially for _____ (name your grandchild), who is struggling with the habit/s of _____ (name them), which is/are not helpful (good, expedient, and profitable for him/her when considered with other things). Father, these habits are symptoms of a flaw in _____'s soul, her character, emotional wounds, needs, and unresolved issues. It isn't healthy or expedient for him/her to habitually make the same mistakes.

I pray that You will bring _____ to the knowledge of truth that will set him/her free. Bring wise counselors across his/her path, Father. Holy Spirit, thank You for causing the Word that he/she has heard to rise up and expose the wrong thought patterns that are driving him/her to continue acting out in ways that are contrary to Your Word.

In the name of Jesus, I bind _____'s spirit, soul, and body to mercy, grace, the blood of Jesus, and the goodness of God, which leads him/her to repentance. I loose ungodly thought patterns, bitterness, unforgiveness, wrong perceptions and attitudes, bad feelings toward others, and a poor self-image from his/her mind. I bind his/her emotions to the control of the Holy Spirit, his/her desires to Your desires, and his/her will to Your will for his/her life.

Thank You, Father, for delivering him/her out of the control of darkness and translating him/her into the kingdom of Your dear Son. He/She is Your garden under cultivation. In the name of Jesus, cause him/her to throw all spoiled virtue and cancerous evil into the garbage. May he/she purpose to let You, the divine gardener, landscape him/her with the Word, making a salvation-garden of his/her life.

Thank You for _____'s salvation and deliverance. I pray that he/she will continually be filled with and controlled by the Holy Spirit.

In the name of Jesus, amen.

Scripture References

Romans 10:9,10	1 Corinthians 10:13
Ephesians 4:21,22 AMP	Ephesians 6:13-17
1 Corinthians 6:12 AMP	1 John 4:4
1 Corinthians 3:9 AMP	2 Corinthians 5:17
James 1:21 MESSAGE	

Prayer for a Teenager

Father, in the name of Jesus, I affirm Your Word over my grandson/granddaughter. I commit _____ to You, knowing that You are able to keep that which I've commited to You against that day. I thank You that You are the deliverer, able to deliver _____ out of rebellion into right relationship with his/her parents and other family members.

Father, the first commandment with a promise is for a child to obey his/her parents in the Lord. You said that all will be well with him/her and he/she will live long on the earth. I affirm this promise on behalf of my grandchild, asking You to give _____ an obedient heart, that he/she may honor (esteem and value as precious) his/her father and mother.

Father, forgive me and his/her parents for mistakes made out of our unresolved hurts or selfishness, which may have caused _____ hurt. I release the anointing that is upon Jesus to bind up and heal this broken heart. Give my grandchild and his/her parents and grandparents the ability to understand and forgive one another, as God for Christ's sake has forgiven us. Thank You for the Holy Spirit, who leads us into all truth and corrects erroneous perceptions about past or present situations.

Thank You for teaching us to listen to each other and giving _____ an ear that hears admonition. I affirm that I will speak excellent and princely things, and the opening of my lips shall be for right things when I talk with him/her. Father, I commit to encourage, guide, and reinforce the godly training and teaching that _____ has received from his/her parents, counselors, and teachers. When _____ is old, he/she will not depart from sound doctrine and teaching, but will follow it all the days of his/her life. In the name of Jesus, I command rebellion to be far from the heart of my grandchild and confess that he/she is willing and obedient, free to enjoy the reward of Your promises. _____ shall be peaceful, bringing peace to others.

Father, according to Your Word, we have been given the ministry of reconciliation, and I release this ministry and the word of reconciliation into this family situation. I refuse to provoke or irritate or fret my grandchild; I will not be hard on him/her lest he/she should become discouraged, feeling inferior and frustrated. In the name of Jesus and by the power of the Holy Spirit, I will not break his/her spirit. Father, I forgive my grandchild for the wrongs he/she has done and stand in the gap until he/she comes to his/her senses and escapes out of the snare of the enemy (rebellion). Thank You for watching over Your Word to perform it, turning and reconciling the heart of the rebellious child to the parents and the hearts of the parents to the child. Thank You for bringing my grandchild back into a healthy relationship with You and with his/her parents and other family members, that our lives might glorify You! Amen.

Scripture References

Psalm 55:12-14	Proverbs 8:6,7
1 Peter 5:7	Proverbs 22:6
Psalm 37:4	Isaiah 1:19
John 14:6	Isaiah 54:13
Ephesians 6:1-3	2 Corinthians 5:18,19
1 John 1:9	Colossians 3:21
Isaiah 61:1	John 20:23
John 16:13	Ezekiel 22:30
Proverbs 15:31	Jeremiah 1:12
Proverbs 13:1	Malachi 4:6

Prayer for Grandchildren in the Armed Forces*

Holy, holy, holy, are You, Lord God Almighty, which was, and is, and is to come. We petition You, according to Psalm 91, for the safety of our grandsons, granddaughters, and all military personnel who are in war-torn countries and on peacekeeping missions.

Our armed forces are not in an afternoon athletic contest that they will walk away from and forget about in a couple of hours. This is for keeps, a life-or-death fight to the finish against the devil and all his angels.

While our troops are fighting terrorists and those who would take away our freedom, we who are praying look beyond human instruments of conflict and address the forces and authorities and rulers of darkness and powers in the spirit world. We are seated in heavenly places in Christ far above the forces of darkness, and as children of the Most High God we enforce the triumphant victory of our Lord Jesus Christ.

We petition heaven to turn our troops into a real peacekeeping force by pouring out the glory of God through our grandsons and granddaughters in the part of the world where they are stationed. Use them as instruments of righteousness to defeat the plans of the devil.

Lord, we plead the blood of Jesus, asking You to manifest Your power and glory. We entreat You on behalf of the citizens in the countries on both sides of this conflict. They have experienced pain and heartache; they are victims of the devil's strategies to steal, kill, and destroy. We pray that they will come to know Jesus, who came to give life and life more abundantly.

We stand in the gap for the people of the war-torn, devil-overrun land. We expect an overflowing of Your goodness and glory in the lives of those for whom we are praying. May they call upon Your name and be saved.

Almighty God, make known Your salvation; openly show Your righteousness in the sight of the nations.

Father, provide for and protect the families of our armed forces. Preserve marriages; cause the hearts of the parents to turn toward their children and the hearts of the children to turn toward their fathers and mothers. We plead the blood of Jesus over our troops and their families. Provide a support system to undergird, uplift, and edify those who have been left to rear children by themselves. Jesus has been made unto these parents wisdom, right-eousness, and sanctification. Through Your Holy Spirit, comfort the lonely and strengthen the weary.

Father, we are looking forward to that day when the whole earth shall be filled with the knowledge of the Lord as the waters cover the sea.

In Jesus' name I pray. Amen.

Scripture References

Ephesians 6:12 MESSAGE   Psalm 98:2 AMP

Colossians 2:15   Malachi 4:6

John 10:10   1 Corinthians 1:30

Ezekiel 22:30   Isaiah 11:9

Acts 2:21

---

* A portion of this prayer was taken from a letter dated January 22, 1996, written by Kenneth Copeland of Kenneth Copeland Ministries in Fort Worth, Texas, and sent to his partners. Used by permission.

To Know Who They Are in Christ

CHILDREN

Father, in the name of Jesus I bind my grandchildren's minds to the mind of Christ that they might hold the thoughts, feelings, and purposes of His heart, and know who they are in Him.

Children

I thank You for my grandchildren and pray for them, asking You, the glorious Father of our Lord Jesus Christ, to give them wisdom to see clearly and really understand who Christ is and all that He has done for them. I pray that their hearts will be flooded with light so that they can see something of the future You have called them to share.

I pray they will live in unbroken fellowship with You for they are Your sons and daughters. They can do all things through Christ who strengthens them.

May they understand that they have been made the righteousness of God in Christ Jesus, and they are brand-new creations in Him. You chose them; they are accepted in the Beloved, redeemed through the blood of Jesus. They are light shining forth in a dark world, and more than conquerors. Thank You for giving them revelation knowledge, revealing that they are an heir and a joint-heir with Jesus, our Messiah, Redeemer, and Lord!

Scripture References

Ephesians 1

Romans 6:11

1 Corinthians 1:30

Ephesians 5:8

Romans 8:1

Galatians 3:26

2 Corinthians 5:7

Romans 8:37

Safety for Missions Trips

by Pat Horton
Personal Prayer Partner for Word Ministries

Dear Grandparent:

As you pray for your grandchild entering the mission field, I encourage you to pray Psalm 91, a foundation for many prayers, especially prayers for those going into enemy territory. Many accounts of miracles during times of great physical and spiritual danger are recorded that can be identified in this Psalm. I recommend speaking Psalm 91 and this prayer daily until it becomes a natural part of your faith confession. Use this for yourself or any family member who is going on a mission trip.

Prayer

Father God, my family and I come rejoicing that You are our God, that we are Your children, and You have given to us an assignment to go forth into all the world and preach the Gospel to every creature.

Thank You that my grandchild _____ (name him/her) has answered the call, and I know that You have equipped him/her and he/she is following Your specific instructions for this time and place. In the name of Jesus our family members come into agreement and bind our minds to the mind of Christ that we might hold the thoughts, feelings, and purposes of His heart as _____ goes to _____ (name the mission field) in His name. We bind _____ to Your wisdom as he/she goes to places that are foreign to him/her. We thank You that Your wisdom leads, guides, and directs _____ in all his/her ways.

Thank You, Holy Spirit, for going before _____ to prepare the way. Thank You for giving him/her power and authority over all the power of the enemy and nothing shall by any means harm him/her.

Help _____ to remember at all times that he/she wrestles not against flesh and blood, but against principalities, against powers, against the rulers of the darkness of this world, against spiritual wickedness in high places. Wherefore he/she takes unto himself/herself the whole armor of God, that he/she may be able to withstand in the evil day, and having done all, to stand. In the name of Jesus, my grandchild shall remain spiritually and mentally alert at all times.

Thank You for protecting _____'s life from the threat of the enemy, and hiding him/her from the conspiracy of the wicked. I loose, smash, crush, and destroy every effect and influence of word curses, witchcraft, voodoo, incantations, and hexes or wrong prayers that have been spoken against him/her and the mission team.

Thank You that every means of transportation that they will use is covered by the blood of Jesus, and You have sent angels to protect them and see to it that everything works properly and that they arrive safely at their appointed destinations.

Thank You that everything they eat and drink is sanctified by prayer and the Word with thanksgiving. Thank You that You have blessed their bread and water and will take sickness out of the midst of them. If they drink any deadly thing it will not hurt them, in the name of Jesus. Bless their food to the nourishment of their bodies and their bodies to Your service.

Thank You for comforting, encouraging, and strengthening their hearts, making them steadfast in every good work. We rely on Your Word, knowing that You will meet all their need according to Your riches in glory through Christ Jesus our Lord.

Scripture References

Mark 16:15	Matthew 18:18
Ephesians 6:12	Luke 10:19
Exodus 23:25	1 Timothy 4:5
2 Timothy 2:17	Philippians 4:19

When Grandchildren Feel Lonely or Unloved

Father, I bring before You my grandchild, _____, who feels abandoned and unloved. I can't fix him/her, but I ask You, Holy Spirit, to comfort _____. Jesus, You were forsaken, and You understand just how _____ feels. I am thankful that You will never, ever leave him/her alone or reject him/her. You are his/her help in this time of loneliness. I know that Your angels are all around him/her.

In the name of Jesus I bind his/her spirit, soul, and body to mercy and truth, to the cross, and to Your grace that is more than enough. I loose from him/her bad feelings toward others and wrong thoughts that exalt themselves above the knowledge of God. I loose negative words that have been spoken to, about, or by him/her.

Although he/she may feel alone, I know that he/she is not alone, for Your Word says that there is nothing that can separate _____ from the love of Christ. My grandchild will come out on top of every circumstance through Jesus' love.

In Jesus' name I pray. Amen.

Scripture References

Deuteronomy 31:8

1 Samuel 30:6

Psalm 34:7

Psalm 37:4

Psalm 46:1

John 3:16

John 16:32

Romans 5:5

Romans 8:35,37

Romans 10:9,10

Romans 12:21

Ephesians 4:31,32

Ephesians 5:1,2

Philippians 4:8

Hebrews 13:5,6

Grandchild's Boyfriend/Girlfriend*

Father, I know that You care about every area of my grandchild's life, especially whom he/she dates. So I believe that _____ (name your grandchild) is blessed with all spiritual blessings in Christ Jesus. Thank You for sending a boyfriend/girlfriend that he/she can grow with, learn from, and have fun with. In the name of Jesus I bind _____'s mind to the mind of Christ and his/her thoughts, feelings, purposes, and desires to Your will so that he/she might fulfill his/her destiny. I loose wrong perceptions about boy/girl love relationships from him/her, and crush strongholds that protect these thoughts that would lead to emotional trauma and grief.

I know that as _____ puts You first and keeps his/her relationship with You close through Your Word and prayer, You will bless this relationship. Help these two young people to communicate with each other so they will have an understanding of the differences in the way men and women think and see things.

Thank You for bringing _____ into my grandchild's life so they can encourage each other to grow closer to You, Father. Help them to be a blessing to each other, contributing something valuable into each other's life. I pray that _____ and his girlfriend/her boyfriend will stay on fire for You and love Jesus more and more, so that they can grow closer to You and minister to other people.

According to Your Word, unruly friends corrupt and destroy good morals. Help my grandchild and his/her friend say no to unruly friends and to have You as their first love. The Holy Spirit will be present to comfort _____ and _____ when no one else can. Help each one achieve contentment in his/her relationship with You. You are their friend when everyone else leaves. I thank You for the Holy Spirit, who will warn them of bad situations and lead them into good situations. Help this young couple not compromise their relationships with You.

Father, help _____ and _____ to be doers of the Word, and to treat each other with purity in their relationship. May they ever keep their relationship in perspective. They are a brother and a sister in the Lord; help them to act accordingly. I pray that their relationship will be a healthy one, bringing growth and maturity to both of their lives. And thank You that _____ and _____ have favor and a good relationship with each other's family. Help them to just relax and develop their friendship.

Father, I pray that _____ and _____ will always listen to Your Voice and that they will always be sensitive to Your Spirit so that they don't set themselves up for a fall. Help each of them to establish sexual, physical, emotional, and intellectual boundaries so they may walk, live, and conduct themselves in a manner worthy of You. Thank You for Your angels who are protecting them from all harm, evil, and danger. Thank You for what You are doing in their lives.

In Jesus' name I pray. Amen.

Scripture References

Psalm 37:4	1 Corinthians 15:33 AMP
Psalm 91:11	Ephesians 1:3
John 14:18	James 1:5,22
Romans 8:14	1 Peter 5:7

---

* Because the Word of God instructs that children should honor and respect their parents, dating—especially for younger teens—should be with parents' permission. See Ephesians 6:1-3.

Grandchild's Future Spouse

Father, I know that You love my grandchild and that I can trust You to perform Your Word in his/her life.

Father, _____ desires a Christian mate. I petition that Your will be done in his/her life, and that he/she enter into that blessed rest by adhering to, trusting in, and relying on You.

Father, You desire that _____ should live a life free from care, that he/she should be content and satisfied in every situation that that he/she is in, and that he/she should not be anxious or worried about anything. You have said that if _____ will delight himself/herself in You, You will give him/her the desires of his/her heart. It is his/her desire to be married to the person You have chosen for him/her.

I pray for _____. Father, especially help him/her to grow in love—Your kind of love. A friend loves at all times, and _____ desires for his/her future spouse to be his/her very best friend and marriage companion. Send a spouse who shares the same love that _____ has for You, someone who will be one in spirit and purpose with him/her.

Father, I trust You to lead _____ and guide him/her by Your Holy Spirit so that when Your perfect time is right, he/she will have the wisdom, discretion, and discernment to know that his/her choice and Yours are the same for his/her life-mate.

In Jesus' name I pray. Amen.

Scripture References

Genesis 2:18-24	Ephesians 5:22-25
Psalm 37:4,5	Philippians 2:2-7
Psalm 130:5	Philippians 4:6,11 AMP
Proverbs 17:17	Colossians 1:9,10
Isaiah 1:19	Colossians 2:9,10 AMP
Matthew 6:33 RSV	Hebrews 4:3,10 AMP

Health and Healing for Grandchildren

Father, in the name of Jesus, I come before You asking You to heal my grandchild, _____, who needs physical and emotional healing. It is written that the prayer of faith will save the sick, and the Lord will raise him up; and if he has committed sins, he will be forgiven. In the name of Jesus, I loose all unforgiveness, resentment, anger, and bad feelings toward anyone from _____.

He/She is Your child, and his/her body is the temple of the Holy Spirit, and he/she desires to be in good health. I bind ____'s thought patterns to the truth, which will make him/her free—both spiritually and naturally (*good eating habits, medications if necessary, and appropriate rest and exercise*). You bought him/her with a price, and he/she will glorify You in his/her body and spirit—they both belong to You.

Thank You, Father, for sending Your Word to heal _____ and deliver him/her from all destructions. Jesus, You are the Word who became flesh and dwelt among us. You bore _____'s griefs (pains) and carried his/her sorrows (sickness). You were pierced through for his/her transgressions and crushed for his/her iniquities, the chastening for his/her well-being fell upon You, and by Your scourging he/she is healed.

Father, I bind _____'s mind to the mind of Christ
and bind his/her desires to Yours for his/her life. _____
gives attention to Your words and inclines his/her ear to
Your sayings. He/She will not let them depart from
his/her sight but will keep them in the midst of his/her
heart, for they are life and health to his/her whole body.

Father, You pardon all _____'s iniquities; You
heal all his/her diseases; You redeem his/her life from the
pit; You crown his/her head with loving-kindness and
compassion; You satisfy his/her years with good things so
that his/her youth is renewed like the eagle's.

Since the Spirit of Him who raised Jesus from the
dead dwells in _____, He will also give life to his/her
mortal body.

Thank You that _____ will prosper and be in
health, even as his/her soul prospers. In Jesus' name I
pray. Amen.

Scripture References

James 5:15 NKJV	Isaiah 53:4,5 NAS
1 Corinthians 6:19,20	Proverbs 4:20-22 NAS
John 8:32	Psalm 103:3-5 NAS
Psalm 107:20	Romans 8:11 NKJV
John 1:14	3 John 2

For Grandchildren To Understand Their Value

Dear Grandparent:

It is vital that your grandchildren see themselves as valuable and precious. They face pressures that we can't imagine from many fronts. Recently I was talking with a group of young people, and they expressed the pressure of having to get into the "rat race" at an early age. They felt driven to be successful and felt inferior if they did not live up to expectations of others.

Talk with your grandchildren, write notes and send cards and e-mails affirming them, and validate their feelings. With prayer as your foundation, you can be an instrument of encouragement, a place of safety for them. You can help launch your grandchildren into their destinies.

Help your grandchildren accept themselves as God made them for His purposes. In his book *Your Best Life Now,* Joel Osteen writes:

> It's vital that you accept yourself and learn to be happy with who God made you to be. If you want to truly enjoy your life, you must be at peace with yourself. Many people constantly feel badly about themselves. They are overly critical of themselves, living with all sorts of self-imposed guilt

and condemnation. No wonder they're not happy; they have a war going on inside. They're not at peace with themselves. And if you can't get along with yourself, you will never get along with other people. The place to start is by being happy with who God made you to be.*

Prayer

Father, I come before the throne of grace to find mercy and grace to help my grandchildren, _____ (name them), in their hour of need.

In the name of Jesus, I receive and welcome these children as gifts from You. They are my reward, and I commit to pray and not give up. I purpose to love them unconditionally and build them up, commending their strengths. Give me the wisdom to hear beyond their words and to help them explore how they can overcome their weaknesses. Father, thank You for the Holy Spirit, who is with them to build them up and show them their value as individuals. Their lives have purpose because You have a special work for them to do for the kingdom of God.

Open the eyes of their understanding, and reveal that it is Your mercy and wonderful kindness that saved them. You raised them from death to life with Christ Jesus, and You have given them a place beside Christ in heaven.

You chose my grandchildren before the foundation of the world to be holy and without blame before You in love; and You appointed them that they should go and bear fruit. You made them what they are; they are Your design. Because You are our God, You will keep them as the apple of Your eye; You will hide them under Your wings.

Scripture References

Hebrews 4:16	Psalm 127:3 NLT
Ephesians 2:4-6 CEV	Ephesians 1:4
John 15:16	Ephesians 2:10
Psalm 17:8	

---

* Joel Osteen, *Your Best Life Now* (New York: Warner Faith, 2004).

Self-Esteem/Appearance

Father, I come to Your throne room in order to receive help for my grandchildren, _____ (name them). You created them with basic needs, and You will supply all their need according to Your riches in glory by Christ Jesus. I pray that no weapon formed against them will prosper, and every tongue that rises against them in judgment they shall show to be in the wrong.

Open the eyes of their understanding, and give them faith to receive Your unconditional love. This love is shed abroad in my heart, and I accept them just as You accepted me. May they be encouraged to excellence, rather than criticized. They can do all things through Christ, who strengthens them. Nothing shall be impossible to them, because they believe You.

You didn't just carelessly or thoughtlessly throw them together. You made them so wonderfully complex! It is amazing to think about. Your workmanship is marvelous— and how well I know it.

My grandchildren are Your workmanship, Your handicraft, made for good works, and You are there to help them view themselves from Your perspective. Open their eyes so they can recognize the strengths, abilities, and talents that You have placed inside of them. Give them grace to find the good that is in them. Help them to be appreciative of who they are, instead of being critical of who they are not.

Knowing that You chose them makes them feel special. Thank You for choosing them before the foundation of the world. I pray that my grandchildren will always acknowledge You, God, as their Father.

May each grow to maturity in relationship with You and develop into the happy, joyful, strong Christian witness that each one has the potential to be.

In Jesus' name I pray. Amen.

Scripture References

Genesis 1:27	Ephesians 2:10 AMP
1 Samuel 16:7	Colossians 3:2
Psalm 139:14	Hebrews 4:16
Isaiah 57:15	1 Peter 2:9
Romans 12:1	1 Peter 4:10
2 Corinthians 6:18	1 John 3:1-3
Ephesians 1:4	

I.

Appearance for Grandsons

Father, I thank You that my grandsons, _____ (name them), shall be mighty upon the earth; they shall walk uprightly before You, and they shall be blessed. They shall not give place to harmful fads but shall be established and steady, led by Your Spirit.

In the name of Jesus, may these grandsons seek first the kingdom of God and Your righteousness (Your ways of doing and being right). Help them learn how to take care of their bodies and to maximize all the natural gifts that You have given to each of them.

In the name of Jesus I bind their minds and attitudes to self-restraint, prudent behavior, and self-discipline. I pray that they will increase in stature and make wise choices about eating and exercise. They shall put their trust in the Lord and refrain from using harmful substances.

Your Word is life to them and health to all their flesh. May they treat their bodies with respect because Your Holy Spirit lives in them.

They are so valuable that You gave Your only Son for their salvation. Thank You for perfecting everything that concerns them.

In Jesus' name I pray. Amen.

Scripture References

Genesis 1:26,27,31

Psalm 37:4,5

Psalm 100:3

Psalm 112

Psalm 139:13,15 AMP

Psalm 149:4

Proverbs 4:20-22

Proverbs 31:30

Isaiah 44:2

John 3:16

John 10:10

1 Corinthians 6:19,20

1 Corinthians 9:25-27 AMP

1 Peter 3:4

1 Peter 5:7

II.

Appearance for Granddaughters

Father, I thank You that my granddaughters,
_____ (name them), are capable, intelligent, and
virtuous (valiant) women. They are far more precious than
jewels, and their value is far above rubies or pearls. They
gird themselves with strength [spiritual, mental, and physical fitness for their God-given tasks] and make their arms
strong and firm.

In the name of Jesus, they shall increase in wisdom
and stature as they seek first the kingdom of God and
Your righteousness (Your ways of doing and being right).
In the name of Jesus, I loose the obsession with weight

from their thought patterns and bind their minds to their God-given love, power, and self-control, so they will choose to eat wisely and exercise properly.

Thank You for helping my granddaughters work out their own salvation. Their bodies are the temples of the Holy Spirit, and they bring glory and honor to You in their spirits and bodies, in the name of Jesus.

Scripture References

Proverbs 31   Matthew 6:33

Matthew 18:18   Philippians 2:12

1 Corinthians 6:19

Protection From Homosexuality

I.

To Develop a Healthy Sexual Identity

Holy Father, my Wonderful Counselor and Prince of Peace, I pray that my grandchildren will desire truth in the inner being and know wisdom in their inmost heart. (Ps. 51:6 AMP.)

Bring their mothers and fathers to maturity, and give them eyes to see the warning signs of gender confusion. Give them the knowledge and wisdom to help these boys and girls develop healthy sexual identities; teaching the boys to embrace their manliness, and the girls their womanliness. I pray that they will not exasperate these vessels of pliable clay to resentment, but will rear them [tenderly] in the training, discipline, counsel, and admonition of the Lord!

In the name of Jesus, I pull down all strongholds of homosexuality and any other perverseness that would try to ensnare my grandchildren. I bind their minds to the mind of Christ, and loose any hint of gender confusion and self-rejection from their thought patterns.

These children shall know the truth about their true sexual identity, and the truth shall make them free to be the men and women You created them to be. They will not dishonor their bodies in the name of Jesus, but will present their bodies to You as living sacrifices. My grandchildren will embrace the truth of God, worship and serve the Creator, who is blessed forever!

Father, You are a wall of fire round about my grandchildren, and the glory within them. Protect them from perverse individuals who are willfully contrary in heart. I pray that the perverse tongue shall be cut down [like a barren and rotten tree], and my grandchildren shall run from all that would corrupt them.

Thank You that my grandchildren will learn from their own experience how their ways will really satisfy You. I declare and decree that my grandsons shall become men of great wisdom and mighty valor; my granddaughters shall become capable, intelligent, virtuous (valiant) women of great worth. Thank You that Psalm 91 is the canopy of protection over my grandchildren, in the name of Jesus. Amen.

Scripture References

Romans 1:27 MESSAGE	Zechariah 2:5
Ephesians 6:4 AMP	Proverbs 11:20
Proverbs 10:31	Matthew 18:18
2 Corinthians 10:3-5	Romans 12:2 TLB

II.

To Overcome a Homosexual Lifestyle

by Kathy Witherell
Member of the Word Ministries Prayer Team

Dear Grandparent:

If you have a grandchild involved in a homosexual lifestyle, I encourage you to maintain your faith in God by praying the following prayer. The Holy Spirit will help you pray and will allow you to see your grandchild from God's perspective. Do not hide yourself from the needs of your own flesh and blood; do not hold this against him/her, but forgive the individual and stand in the gap before God for his/her deliverance. Love him/her unconditionally with the love of the Lord.

Prayer

Dear God, bring Your love and acceptance into the empty places in the life of my grandchild, _____ (name your grandchild). This void he/she is trying to fill has opened the door for the father of lies to captivate and trick him/her into believing a lie. This deception and crisis of gender identification and orientation has become a stronghold.

In the name of Jesus I crush, smash, and annihilate this stronghold and call my grandchild out of Satan's grip and into Your strong hand of love and protection. I bind his/her mind to the mind of Christ, his/her will to the will of God, his/her plans to Your plans. Lord, You plan to prosper _____ and will not harm him/her; You plan to give him/her a hope and a future. _____ will call upon You, and You will listen; he/she will seek You and find You when he/she seeks You with all his/her heart, and You will bring him/her out of this relationship and situation.

I bind him/her to mercy, truth, the blood of Jesus, and the work of Jesus on the cross. I loose, untie, and smash self-rejection, every lie, thoughts of false identity, and the deception of Satan's schemes.

Let my grandchild see that only Jesus can fulfill his/her need for beauty and intimacy in his/her life. I command the light that shines out of darkness to shine in his/her heart. Let him/her see who You really made him/her to be in Christ. Replace his/her ignorance with the accurate knowledge of Your Word; expose the counterfeit and the utter darkness it brings.

Send reliable, proven Christian support to him/her. I pray that the Spirit of life in Christ Jesus will make him/her free from the law of sin and death. Give him/her a hunger for true life in You, for I know that Jesus, Your precious Son, is the way, the truth, and the life. In His name I pray. Amen.

Scripture References

John 8:44	2 Timothy 2:26
2 Corinthians 10:3-5	Matthew 18:18
Jeremiah 29:11,12	2 Corinthians 4:3-6
Romans 8:2	John 14:6

Breaking Generational Curses

Father, I bring my family before the throne of grace as a living memorial. I am strong in You and the power of Your might. You planted me like a strong and graceful oak for Your own glory and anointed me to rebuild the ancient ruins, reviving them though they have lain there many generations. You forgave all our iniquities, and in the name of Jesus I repent and renounce my sins and the sins of my ancestors, asking You to forgive us and cleanse us from all unrighteousness.

Forgive us for exalting family culture, customs, and traditions above the Word of God, and loving the world more than we love You. Forgive us for being stiff-necked, stubborn, and rebellious, and for insisting on having our own way. I repent of and renounce cynicism, selfishness, and self-centeredness. Forgive us for teaching and training our children to please men rather than You, for planting and fostering in them the fear of rejection, failure, abandonment, and judgment. Forgive us for entertaining lying spirits and winking at sin. I repent of our sins, the sins of our forefathers back to the third and fourth generations, and I renounce the spirit of antichrist that has been at work in our families on both the paternal and maternal sides.

Father, by faith we forgive those who have trespassed against us, for they did not know what they were doing; and we ask You to forgive us our trespasses, which have separated us from Your love, from ourselves, and from one another.

In the name of Jesus, I use powerful weapons of warfare to tear down, annihilate, crush, and smash strongholds (vain imaginations and warped philosophies) handed down from our forefathers. I capture and bring into obedience mindsets that are in opposition to the Word of God. I break, smash, and annihilate the generational curses of our earthly fathers, and I bow before You, Jesus.

Lord, thank You for bringing us out from under doom by taking the curse for our wrongdoing upon Yourself. Heavenly Father, You are faithful, forgiving, loving, kind, compassionate, and full of mercy.

Scripture References

Colossians 1:13 AMP	Luke 10:19
Ephesians 6:10	Isaiah 61:3,4
Psalm 103:3	1 John 1:9
Psalm 78:8	Hebrews 13:6
Exodus 20:5	Matthew 6:14
2 Corinthians 10:4,5	Galatians 3:13 NLT
Psalm 145:8	

Soul-Ties*

Lord, my grandchild, _____(name him/her), has been looking to another human being to fix the need and the pain inside of him/her. In Jesus' name, I forgive him/her for not keeping his/her relationship with this person in proper perspective. Jesus, You came to set him/her free from every emotional, intellectual, or self-willed tie he/she has let form. Thank You for bringing him/her to the place of repentance. I stand in the gap for him/her, forgiving my grandchild for seeking satisfaction and fulfillment from anyone other than You.

In the name of Jesus I loose, cut, and sever any and all soul-ties he/she has willingly or ignorantly entered into. Open the eyes of his/her understanding, and give him/her the courage to reject these soul-ties and every soulish satisfaction they have provided for him/her. In the name of Jesus, I loose them from his/her mind and emotions. I renounce every wrong agreement my grandchild has ever come into that birthed these soul-ties in the first place.

I bind him/her to the truth of Your love, care, faithfulness, mercy, and grace. Your grace is sufficient for all his/her needs, hurts, and issues. Thank You for giving him/her the courage to trust You and the wisdom and understanding necessary to bring his/her needs and vulnerabilities to You alone. I tear down, crush, smash, and annihilate the stronghold of fear that overcomes my grandchild when he/she feels defenseless and vulnerable.

Thank You for drawing my grandchild to Yourself with cords and bands of love and leading him/her to repentance by Your goodness. I praise You for binding up his/her brokenness and meeting his/her needs. Jesus, I declare that You are Lord over my family.

Scripture References

Galatians 5:1	Ezekiel 22:30
Ephesians 1:18	Matthew 16:19
2 Corinthians 12:9	Hosea 11:4 AMP
Ezekiel 34:16	Romans 10:9,10

---

* Based on the prayer written by Liberty Savard "Training Wheel Prayer for Breaking Soul-Ties" in *Breaking the Power* (North Brunswick, NJ: Bridge-Logos, 1997), pp. 171-172.

To Overcome the Battle in Their Mind

Father, I take my stand and will do all to stand on behalf of my grandchildren. They live in this unprincipled, dog-eat-dog world. The world doesn't fight fair. But I don't live or fight my battles that way—never have and never will. The tools of my trade aren't for marketing or manipulation, but they are for demolishing that entire massively corrupt culture that would try to squeeze the minds of my grandchildren into its mold. I use my powerful God-tools for smashing warped philosophies, tearing down barriers erected against Your truth, and fitting every loose thought and emotion and impulse of my grandchildren into the structure of life shaped by Christ. My tools are ready at hand for clearing the ground of every obstruction and building their lives of obedience into maturity.

No matter where my grandchildren go, Your Spirit will go with them to convict and convince them of sin, righteousness, and judgment. I call each and every grandchild out of darkness into light, and I pray that they will no longer follow the course and fashion of this world. The prince of the power of the air has been defeated, and he shall not have control over their minds, in the name of Jesus.

Father, You see the battle that is being fought for their minds. I bind their minds to the mind of Christ, and I bind them—spirit, soul, and body—to the cross, to the mercy and grace of God. I loose thoughts of inferiority and self-hatred and any other wrong, perverse thinking from their thought patterns and attitudes. Holy Spirit, cause the Word that they have heard to rise in each of them. They shall know the truth, and the truth shall make my grandchildren, _____ (name them), free from the law of the spirit of sin and death.

I decree that they shall no longer be conformed to this world, but shall be transformed by the entire renewing of their minds so they can know the will of God. God of peace, I ask You to sanctify these precious children through and through [separate them from profane things, make them pure and wholly consecrated to Yourself]; and may their spirits and souls and bodies be preserved sound and complete [and found] blameless at the coming of our Lord Jesus Christ (the Messiah).

Scripture References

2 Corinthians 10:3-6   Psalm 139:7-9

  MESSAGE   Ephesians 2:1,2

Matthew 18:18   Romans 12:2

1 Thessalonians 5:23

Dealing With Divorce and Remarriage

I.

Healing From the Pain of Divorce

Dear Grandparent:

God doesn't like divorce, but He loves divorced people. God doesn't like sexual immorality, but He loves unwed parents. Remember that the Father forgives (1 John 1:9), and that it is important that we forgive our adult children and/or their spouses when they make unwise choices. God is merciful, and He is the God of the second chance. Remember that God may not approve of our behavior, but He approves and accepts us—not because of what we've done or haven't done, but because of what Christ has done for us. "Open up before God, keep nothing back; he'll do whatever needs to be done: He'll validate your life in the clear light of day and stamp you with approval at high noon" (Ps. 37:5,6 MESSAGE).

Put away bitterness, fear, and resentment toward your child and his/her spouse. When talking with your grand-children, do not allow yourself to condemn and blame others for what has happened. Pursue peace; minister reconciliation and hope. Don't minimize or maximize the wrong others have done; do not attack the person. Admit where you or others may have been wrong or at fault, and be honest with yourself and them.

Do not talk with scorn or disrespect about the one who is not present for your grandchildren. When you talk with your grandchildren, speak the truth in love rather than tearing down and destroying a possible harmonious relationship with an absent parent. (Eph. 4:15.) If your grandchild does not know who his/her biological dad is, talk with him/her about his heavenly Father in loving terms, affirming him/her and reinforcing his/her self-worth.

The age of your grandchildren will determine what they are able to hear and bear. In John 16:12 NLT, Jesus said to His disciples, "Oh, there is so much more I want to tell you, but you can't bear it now." Don't overburden your grandchildren, but lean on the wisdom of the Holy Spirit to speak a word in due season.

Prayer

Lord, in the name of Jesus, I approach Your throne of grace with confidence, so that I may receive mercy and find grace to help my family in our time of need. Father, You are a merciful God; You will not abandon my daughter/son and grandchildren.

In the name of Jesus, I forgive my debtors, including those who have offended, rejected, or abandoned my grandchildren, or otherwise caused them pain and suffering. Holy Spirit, I call on You to give me the words to explain to my grandchildren why their mom/dad does not live with them. I purpose to be honest with my grandchildren [speaking truly, dealing truly, and living truly], telling them only that which they can bear, that which is appropriate according to their ages.

Lord, give ear to my voice when I cry out to You. Let my prayer be set before You as incense, the lifting up of my hands as the evening sacrifice. Set a guard, O Lord, over my mouth; keep watch over the door of my lips.

Help me to listen with an open heart, recognizing my grandchildren's hurt and anger—even their self-blame. Holy Spirit, give me words of comfort when we talk, and help me answer their questions with grace-filled words. Prepare their hearts to hear when I share why they are not living in a two-parent home.

Father, You are a present help in the midst of trouble. You will never leave my grandchildren or forsake them. Father, I believe that all things work together and are [fitting into a plan] for good because we love You and are called according to Your design and purpose.

In the name of Jesus I pray. Amen.

Scripture References

Hebrews 4:16 NIV

Deuteronomy 4:31 NIV

Matthew 6:12 NIV

Ephesians 4:15 AMP

Psalm 141:1-3 NKJV

Psalm 46:1

Hebrews 13:5

Romans 8:28 AMP

II.

To Discuss Remarriage With Your Grandchildren

Dear Grandparents:

In order to discuss this subject with your grandchildren, you need wisdom, answers for their questions, and good communication skills. I encourage you to pray the previous prayers and meditate on the Scriptures listed. Praying scriptural prayers will prepare you to deal with issues that are very real. I encourage you to gather information that will give you insight and wisdom.

Prayer does not relieve you of the responsibility to learn all you can about the issues your grandchildren will be facing, but it does prepare your heart and mind to resolve conflicts and issues as they arise. Give this prayer and the previous prayer place in your thoughts, because this is a traumatic event in the lives of your grandchildren.*

Pray that the parent(s) and the soon-to-be spouse will seek wise counsel. "Wisdom is the principal thing; therefore get wisdom. And in all your getting, get understanding" (Prov. 4:7 NKJV). I encourage you to read 1 Corinthians 7 and ask the Holy Spirit to give you insight as you ponder Paul's discussion of marriage and remarriage.

Prayer

Holy Spirit, before I talk with my grandchildren about remarriage, search our hearts, for You know what the mind of the Spirit is, because You make intercession for us according to the will of God. And I know that all things work together for good to those who love God, to those who are the called according to His purpose.

Father, after my son's/daughter's divorce he/she felt as though he/she had been carried into exile, but You healed him/her and brought him/her back to You with cords and bands of unconditional love. His/Her heart has grown content, but now he/she believes that it is Your plan that he/she remarry. It is my desire to see my grandchildren and their dad/mom go out with joy, and be led with peace. The mountains and the hills will break forth into singing before them, and all the trees of the field will clap their hands.

Go before any discussion that I might have with my grandchildren, and prepare their hearts to hear. O Lord, give them a heart to understand, and give me the wisdom to choose my words wisely.

In the name of Jesus, my grandchildren's parents have made their plans, but from You, Lord, comes the wise reply of the tongue. Father, thank You for feeding each one of us like a shepherd, and for gathering my grandchildren and their parents with Your arm, carrying them in Your bosom, and gently leading all of us who will be discussing remarriage with them.

In the name of Jesus, I present this request. Amen.

Scripture References

Proverbs 4:7 NKJV	Isaiah 55:12 NKJV
1 Corinthians 7:1-39 NIV	Proverbs 16:1 NIV
Romans 8:27,28 NKJV	Isaiah 40:11 NKJV
Hosea 11:4	

---

* "Along with the dream of living in a two-parent home, every child of divorce clings to the dream that the natural parents will somehow reunite. When the mom or dad remarries, that effectively destroys the dream of reunion." Dr. Frank Minirty, Dr. Brian Newman, and Dr. Paul Warren, *The Father Book: An Instruction Manual* (Nashville, TN: Thomas Nelson, Inc., 1992), p. 239.

The College Years

Dear Grandparent:

Several years ago when our children were in college, their Christian beliefs were challenged, especially in their religion and philosophy classes. But God's Word is reliable: "Train up a child in the way he should go [and in keeping with his individual gift or bent], and when he is old he will not depart from it" (Prov. 22:6 AMP). Resist the temptation to worry, and hold fast to your confession of faith for your grandchildren so that truth may prevail and God may be glorified in their lives.

Prayer

Father, I pray for _____ (name your grandchild), who is away at college. Thank You that he/she is Your [own] handiwork (Your workmanship), re-created in Christ Jesus, [born anew] that he/she may do those good works which You predestined [planned beforehand] for him/her [taking paths which You prepared ahead of time], that he/she should walk in them [living the good life which You prearranged and made ready for _____ to live].

In the name of Jesus I resist the temptation to worry, and I rest on Your promise because You know the plans

You have for my grandchild. They are plans for good and not for disaster, to give him/her a future and a hope.

I pray that _____ will always let You lead him/her, and You will clear the road for him/her to follow.

You have begun a good work in _____, and I am confident of this very thing: that You will perform it until the day of Jesus Christ.

Thank You for hearing and answering my prayer in the name of Jesus.

Scripture References

Ephesians 2:10 AMP

Proverbs 3:6 CEV

Jeremiah 29:11 NLT

Philippians 1:6 KJV

Protection From Abuse

Dear Grandparent:

Abuse is a subject that cannot be ignored because we are living in perilous times. Surround your grandchildren with scriptural prayers for their protection. Listen to the Word of the Lord: "For thus says the Lord: Even the captives of the mighty will be taken away, and the prey of the terrible will be delivered; for I will contend with him who contends with you, and I will give safety to your children and ease them" (Isa. 49:25 AMP). This includes your grandchildren. God will not fail to fulfill one word of His promises.

There are predators who seek out small children. Watch and pray. If you are a grandparent of a child of abuse, I encourage you to turn to the One who is able to take wicked devices and turn them to work for good. The Holy Spirit will bear you and your family up; He will bring healing. When you don't know what to pray or how to pray as you ought, the Spirit Himself will go to meet your supplication and plead in your behalf with unspeakable yearnings and groanings too deep for utterance. The Holy Spirit is an Intercessor who cannot fail. He will intercede and plead before God on behalf of your grandchild according to and in harmony with God's will. "We know that in everything God works for good with those

who love him, who are called according to his purpose"
(Rom. 8:28 RSV).

Prayer

Heavenly Father, I ask You to protect my grandchildren from physical violence, verbal abuse, and neglect. I
pray that all their needs will be met—proper shelter, food,
clothing, medical treatment—and may they always have
the needed emotional support. In the name of Jesus I
crush, smash, annihilate, and curse any form of child
pornography, incest, or sexual molestation that Satan
would try to devise against these grandchildren. I bind my
grandchildren's feet to the paths of righteousness for Your
name's sake, and I ask You, Lord, to be a wall of fire
round about them, and be the glory in the midst of them.

In the name of Jesus, my elder Brother and Redeemer,
I proclaim the canopy of Psalm 91 over my grandchildren.
Cover them with Your pinions, and under Your wings
shall they trust and find refuge; Your truth and Your faithfulness are a shield and a buckler. I praise You, Lord of
hosts; You shall defend and protect my grandchildren. I do
not ask that You take them out of the world, but that You
keep and protect them from the evil one. In Jesus' name I
pray. Amen.

Scripture References

Zechariah 2:5	Psalm 91:4
Zechariah 9:15	John 17:15

Character

by Janet Blackwell
Member of the Word Ministries Prayer Team

Father, Your Word declares that children are a heritage
and reward from You. As I observe growth and development in my grandchildren, I am encouraged that they are
safe in Your hands. I thank You for every opportunity to
instill tidbits of godly living in these precious ones. Help
me to remember that they won't learn everything in one
day, but that it is a molding and making process overseen
by the divine Potter. Father, let the work of my hands, the
words of my mouth, and the influence of my character
hallow Your name.

O God, I see so much right in my grandchildren. I
don't always like what they wear, nor am I very appreciative of their idea of fun. I often don't understand their
vocabulary, and sometimes I would rather they would
choose more godly friends. So Father, help me work with
You to instill good character in these dear ones. Wisdom
is a good inheritance, better than any material goods I
could ever bestow upon them. Wisdom is their defense, a
protective barrier in their lives. I declare all Your words
over them, Father. Give them the knowledge of Jesus so
that wisdom can do its work in their lives. Teach them to
delight in Your Word, Father, meditating on it day and

night. Let them be like trees planted by rivers of water, bringing forth fruit in their season and not withering. May every characteristic of godliness in their lives prosper.

I thank You, Father, that though these young ones stumble as they are maturing, Your mercies are new every morning. Jesus, abide in them as they abide in You, for You are the vine and they are the branches. Prune them in mercy and grace that they may grow in fruitfulness.

Display the fruit of Your Spirit in them, Father. Let love, joy, and peace replace strife and contentiousness. Overflow their hearts with longsuffering, kindness, and goodness to push out independence, self-reliance, and impatience. Help them in the midst of the trials of life to be faithful. Make their presence in this life sweet with gentleness and self-control because they can trust You completely.

Father, when others see Your children [walking in the way of piety and virtue], the work of Your hands in their midst, they will revere Your name and reverently fear the God of Israel. Those who err in spirit will come to understanding, and those who murmur [discontentedly] will accept instruction.

Bless You, our unchanging Father, who is ever faithful.

Scripture References

Psalm 127:3 NKJV

Psalm 1:2,3

John 15:2

Isaiah 29:23,24

Ecclesiastes 7:12

Lamentations 3:23

Galatians 5:22,23

Operating in Spiritual Gifts

Dear Grandparent:

The gifts of the spirit are not for church services alone but are given to you to help you in your everyday life. Once when our son ran away from home, the Holy Spirit gave my husband a word of knowledge that led us directly to David. My husband calmly opened the car door and said, "David, get in the car. We're going home." This gift profited our entire family. All the gifts abide within you, and the Holy Spirit is always present to help you in your time of need.

Prayer

Father, in the name of Jesus, I come behind in no gift. Thank You for the Holy Spirit, who abides within me to give me aid and support. I welcome Him and acknowledge Him in everything that I do. I need the spiritual gifts working in my life as I pray for my grandchildren and pursue healthy relationships with them.

I pray that my everyday living will be steeped in and guided by the God-kind of love. I earnestly desire, seek, and cultivate the spiritual endowments (gifts), especially that I may prophesy, interpreting Your divine will and purpose in my prayers for my grandchildren; and I pray that my communication with them will be inspired.

In the name of Jesus, I bind my mind to the mind of Christ concerning my grandchildren and my emotions to the control of the Holy Spirit. It is my desire to excel in the gifts that will build up my grandchildren as they pursue their destinies. Thank You, Father, that the gifts of the Spirit are in operation in my life. Father, here in these last days, on the authority of Your Word, I proclaim that You are pouring out Your Spirit on my sons and grand-sons, my daughters and granddaughters, and they will prophesy. They shall come behind in no gift after the Holy Spirit has come upon them.

They shall make Your name to be remembered in all generations; therefore, shall the people praise and give You thanks forever and ever.

Scripture References

1 Corinthians 14   1 Corinthians 1:7

Acts 2:16

Substance Abuse

Dear Grandparent:

This prayer addresses two different types of drug use. The first part of the prayer concerns the young person's use of medication for health problems, as well as the use of medications, such as steroids, to increase strength and virility. The remainder of the prayer is for a child dealing with an addiction.

If your grandchild is an addict, you must avoid being an enabler but must be available to the child in loving, healthy ways. Ask God for His wisdom when you talk with your grandchild. Reasoning with him/her will not work; you are not talking to the person but to the addiction, which has become a stronghold. However, loving prayer does work! Our son was gloriously delivered from drugs after twenty-eight years of addiction, and now he is in the ministry.

Prayer

Father, in the mighty name of Jesus, I come boldly to Your throne of grace that I may obtain mercy and find grace to help in my grandchild's time of need. I believe that You can deliver _____ and protect him/her from every evil.

Give my grandchild and his/her parents the knowledge and wisdom they need concerning any prescribed medications. Alert them to the danger of using steroids simply for better performance and physical appearance. Give them the grace to speak up and take responsibility for _____'s healthcare, and to say "no" to the abuse of medications. Lead them by Your Spirit to the right doctors, beginning with the pediatricians. May they not search for a quick fix for symptoms, but find the root cause (genetic, physiological, and/or spiritual) of the problem.

Lord, it will give me great joy when my grandchildren are walking in truth. I pray for _____, who has been called an addict. Set him/her free from alcohol/drugs/tobacco/other addictions. _____ can't do it alone; he/she needs Your help. I loose wrong thought patterns and attitudes from him/her: bad feelings toward others, a poor self-image, hopelessness, confusion, unforgiveness, depression, and thoughts of suicide. I break the power of word curses that have been spoken to, about, or by him/her. I ask You to cause the Word that he/she has heard to arise within him/her. You alone can fill the void in his/her heart.

In the name of Jesus, I bind _____ to Your grace and mercy and to the blood of Jesus. I bind his/her thoughts to truth so that he/she will call upon the name of the Lord and be saved from his/her destructions.

Father, You are faithful. You will not allow _____ to be tempted beyond his/her powers of endurance. In every temptation, You will always show him/her a way out. I bind _____'s feet to paths of righteousness for Your name's sake, that he/she will determine not to go to the wrong types of parties or places that make it easier to give in to alcohol/drugs/tobacco and other addictions. Your goodness leads _____ to repentance, and I see him/her born again, filled with Your Spirit, and walking in victory. Father, the thoughts that You think toward _____ are thoughts of peace and not of evil, to give him/her a future and a hope.

Thank You, Lord, for an addiction-free life for _____. Holy Spirit, I thank You for guiding him/her to godly counselors, friends, and a Christ-centered support group. In Jesus' name I pray. Amen.

Scripture References

Hebrews 4:14-16

Psalm 107:20

1 Corinthians 10:13
    PHILLIPS

Romans 2:4

Jeremiah 29:11

3 John 4

James 4:7

1 Corinthians 15:33,34

Galatians 5:18-21

Ephesians 5:18

Provision

You are Jehovah-Jireh, the One who sees the needs of my grandchildren, and You are their provider just as You have been mine. I will make Your name to be remembered in all generations; therefore shall my grandchildren praise and give You thanks forever.

In the name of Jesus my grandchildren shall be good financial stewards, give tithes and offerings, and budget their money wisely. They hearken unto Your voice, and all spiritual and material blessings shall come on them and overtake them. Hallelujah! I have never seen the righteous forsaken, nor his seed begging bread. May Your name be hallowed in the lives of my grandchildren. Thank You for supplying our every need.

God, You are able to make all grace (every favor and earthly blessing) come to my grandchildren in abundance, so that they may always and under all circumstances and whatever the need be self-sufficient [possessing enough to require no aid or support and furnished in abundance for every good work and charitable donation]. You are watching over Your Word to perform it. Hallelujah! Praise the name of the Lord!

Scripture References

Matthew 6:33 NKJV   Deuteronomy 28:2

Psalm 45:17 AMP   2 Corinthians 9:8 AMP

To Walk in Faith and Power

Father, I thank You that my grandchildren received power when the Holy Spirit came upon them and they shall be Your witnesses at home and abroad.

In the name of Jesus I do not cease to give thanks for _____ (name your grandchildren), making mention of them in my prayers: that You, the God of our Lord Jesus Christ, the Father of glory, may give to them the spirit of wisdom and revelation in the knowledge of our Lord and Savior, Jesus Christ. Open the eyes of their understanding concerning the exceeding greatness of Your power toward them—the power that raised Jesus from the dead.

Father, thank You for dealing to each of my grandchildren a measure of faith. By grace they have been saved through faith, and they live by the faith of the Son of God, who loves them and gave His life for them. They are strong in You, Lord, and in the power of Your might.

They are being strengthened with might through the Spirit in the inner man that Christ may dwell in their hearts through faith. I decree that they are rooted and grounded in love, able to comprehend with all the saints what is the width and length and depth and height—to know the love of Christ which passes knowledge; that they may be filled with all the fullness of God.

You are able to do exceedingly abundantly above all that they ask or think according to the power that works in them.

Scripture References

Acts 1:8

Romans 12:3

Galatians 2:20

Ephesians 3:16-20

Ephesians 1:16-20

Ephesians 2:8

Ephesians 6:10

Salvation of Grandchildren

Father, I come before You bearing the names of my grandchildren upon my heart, bringing them in continual remembrance before You as living memorials. I ask You, Lord of the harvest, to raise up and send the perfect laborer to each one to share the gospel in a way that they will hear and understand. Father, thank You for bringing them to repentance by Your goodness and love. Through prayer my grandchildren's hearts are prepared, and they will not be able to resist the wooing of the Holy Spirit.

Your Spirit is wherever they may go, present to convict and convince them of sin, righteousness, and judgment. They can never be lost to Your Spirit!

Father, I use Your mighty weapons to knock down the devil's strongholds that would try to keep my grandchildren from hearing and comprehending truth. In the name of Jesus, I break down these strongholds and every proud argument that would keep them from knowing You. With these weapons I conquer rebellious ideas and teach my grandchildren to obey truth.

My grandchildren shall confess that Jesus is Lord and shall turn from darkness to light, from Satan to You.

In the name of Jesus, I forgive their sin and stand in the gap before You for _____ (name your grandchildren).

By faith I thank You now for their salvation and redemption. Jesus is Lord over my family!

Scripture References

Exodus 28:29	2 Corinthians 5:19
Romans 10:9,10	John 16:8,9
1 John 1:9	Romans 5:8
2 Corinthians 5:17	John 14:6
John 3:16	Romans 10:13
John 6:37	Ephesians 2:1-10
John 10:10	John 1:12
Romans 3:23	2 Corinthians 5:21

Grandchildren To Be Filled With the Spirit

Father, thank You for choosing my grandchildren before the foundation of the world. They shall confess Jesus as Lord because they will believe in their hearts that You raised Him from the dead.

It is witten that when we repent and are baptized in the name of Jesus Christ for the remission of our sins, we shall receive the gift of the Holy Spirit. You made this promise to us and to our children and their children. I believe that they shall prophesy and You shall pour out Your Spirit on them.

Jesus said, "How much more shall your heavenly Father give the Holy Spirit to those who ask Him!" (Luke 11:13). When my children and grandchildren ask You to fill them with the Holy Spirit, they shall be filled. Thank You for leading them into the fullness and power that You have for them in the name of Jesus. I affirm that they are Spirit-filled Christians and they will speak in other tongues as the Spirit gives them utterance. Praise the Lord! Amen.

Scripture References

Romans 10:9,10

John 14:16,17

Luke 11:13

Acts 1:8

Acts 2:4

Acts 2:32,33,39

Acts 8:12-17

Acts 10:44-46

Acts 19:2,5,6

Romans 10:9,10

1 Corinthians 14:2-15

1 Corinthians 14:18,27

Ephesians 6:18

Jude 1:20

Part 3

PERSONAL PRAYERS

Beginning Each Day

Father, as the _____ (owner, president, chairman, manager, supervisor) of _____ (name of company), I come before You rejoicing, for this is the day which You have made and I will be glad in it. Obedience is better than sacrifice, so I am making a decision to submit to Your will today, that my plans and purposes may be conducted in a manner that will bring honor and glory to You. Cause me to be spiritually and mentally alert in this time of meditation and prayer.

It is into Your keeping that I place my family—my parents, spouse, children, and grandchildren—knowing that You are able to keep that which I commit to You against that day. Thank You for the angels that You have commanded concerning me and my family to guard us in all our ways; they will lift us up in their hands so that we will not strike our foot against a stone.

Thank You, Lord, for the tremendous success that my associates and I have experienced in our organization and for the increase in profits and productivity we have enjoyed. Thank You for Your faithfulness to us day by day and for helping us to become all that You desire us to be.

Thank You, Father, for helping to make us a company that continues to grow and expand. We recognize that without Your help, it would not be possible. Without

Your direction and guidance, we would fail; with it we can prosper and have good success. I continue to thank You for the many blessings that You have poured out upon us all.

I especially thank You for the co-laborers with whom I will be interacting today. Give me words of wisdom, words of grace, that I might encourage them and build them up.

Father, I kneel before You, from whom Your whole family in heaven and on earth derives its name. I pray that out of Your glorious riches You may strengthen each one with power through Your Spirit in the inner being, so that Christ may dwell in each heart through faith.

Now to Him who is able to do immeasurably more than all we ask or imagine, according to His power that is at work within us, to Him be the glory in this company and in Christ Jesus throughout all generations, for ever and ever! In Jesus' name I pray. Amen.

Scripture References

Psalm 118:24	Lamentations 3:22,23
1 Samuel 15:22	Joshua 1:8
2 Timothy 1:12	Ephesians 3:14-17 NIV
Psalm 91:11,12 NIV	Ephesians 3:20 NIV

Praise and Thanksgiving

Father, I love You with all my strength, spirit, soul, and body. I come to praise You, Lord of lords, King of kings, Redeemer, Prince of Peace, Almighty God. I thank You for Your goodness and Your love. I'll continually thank You for Your mercy, which endures forever.

I praise You, Lord, and I will not forget all Your benefits. Thank You for forgiving my sins and for healing all my diseases. You fill my life with good things.

Father, You created the heavens, the earth, the sea, and everything in them. Thank You for making me so I can enjoy life to the fullest. This is the day that You have made, and I rejoice and am glad in it. You are my strength and my joy.

I thank You and praise You for supplying and providing everything I need. You are all-powerful, You know everything, and You are everywhere. Thank You for being such a loving Father to me and giving Jesus to be my Savior, Lord, and friend. Thank You for sending the Holy Spirit to fill me, guide me, comfort me, and teach me the right things to do.

I'll praise You in everything.

In Jesus' name I pray. Amen.

Scripture References

Psalms 18:30; 24:1; 28:7;
34:1; 48:1; 63:3,4,5;
71:8; 103:2,3,5,8;
106:1; 118:24; 136:1

Nehemiah 8:10

Philippians 4:19

John 10:10; 14:16 AMP

Revelation 4:8,11

To Pray

Father, in the name of Jesus, I thank You for calling me to be a fellow workman—a joint promoter and a laborer together—with You. I commit to pray and not to give up.

Jesus, You are the Son of God, and I will never stop trusting You. You are my High Priest, and You understand my weaknesses. So I come boldly to the throne of my gracious God. There I receive mercy and find grace to help when I need it.

There are times I do not know what I ought to pray for. Holy Spirit, I submit to Your leadership and thank You for interceding for us with groans that words cannot express. You search hearts and know the mind of the spirit, because You intercede for the saints in accordance with God's will.

Therefore, I am assured and know that (with God being a partner in my labor) all things work together and are [fitting into a plan] for my good, because I love God and am called according to [His] design and purpose.

I resist the temptation to be anxious about anything, but in every circumstance and in everything by prayer and petition [definite requests] with thanksgiving I continue to make my wants (and the wants of others) known to

God. Whatever I ask for in prayer, I believe that it is granted to me, and I will receive it.

You made Christ, who never sinned, to be the offering for our sin, so that we could be made right with You through Christ. Now my earnest (heartfelt, continued) prayer makes tremendous power available—dynamic in its working. Father, I live in You—abide vitally united to You—and Your words remain in me and continue to live in my heart. Therefore, I ask whatever I will, and it shall be done for me. When I produce much fruit, I bring great glory to my Father—the Father of my Lord Jesus Christ. Amen.

Scripture References

1 Corinthians 3:9 NIV

Luke 18:1 NIV

Romans 8:26,27 NIV

Romans 8:28 AMP

Philippians 4:6 AMP

Mark 11:24 AMP

2 Corinthians 5:21 NLT

James 5:16 AMP

John 15:7,8 AMP

To Trust in the Lord

Heavenly Father, You are my God and early will I seek You, knowing that You hear the cry of the righteous. You are my hope, sovereign Lord. You are my confidence, and You will keep my foot from being snared. I have been made the righteousness of God in Christ Jesus, and my prayers avail much.

Jesus is the way into the Holy of Holies and the High Priest of my confession. I have confidence to enter the Most Holy Place by the blood of Jesus. In Christ Jesus and through faith in Him I approach You, my Father, with freedom and confidence. If I ask anything according to Your will, You hear me. And if I know that You hear me, whatever I ask, I know that I have what I have asked of You.

On the authority of Your Word, I believe that when I do not know what I ought to pray for, the Holy Spirit Himself intercedes for me with groans that words cannot express. He searches my heart, knowing the mind of the Spirit, and intercedes for me in accordance with Your will. And I know that in all things You are working for my good because I love You. You called me according to Your purpose; You chose me before the foundation of the world to be holy and without blame before You in love.

In the name of Jesus, I will not throw away my confidence; it will be richly rewarded. I will persevere so that when I have done Your will, I will receive what You have promised. I am Your righteous one who is living by faith in the name of Jesus. Amen.

Scripture References

Psalm 63:1 NKJV	Hebrews 3:1 NAS
Psalm 34:17	Hebrews 10:19-25 NLT
Psalm 55:17,18	1 John 5:14,15 NKJV
Psalm 71:5	Romans 8:26-28 NIV
Proverbs 3:26 NIV	Ephesians 1:4
1 Corinthians 1:30	Hebrews 10:35,36 NIV
James 5:16	Galatians 2:20

To Walk in the Word

Father, in the name of Jesus, I commit myself to walk in the Word. Your Word living in me produces Your life in this world. I recognize that Your Word is integrity itself—steadfast, sure, eternal—and I trust my life to its provisions.

You have sent Your Word forth into my heart. I let it dwell in me richly in all wisdom. I meditate in it day and night so that I may diligently act on it. The incorruptible seed, the living Word, the Word of truth, is abiding in my spirit. That seed is growing mightily in me now, producing Your nature, Your life. It is my counsel, my shield, my buckler, my powerful weapon in battle. The Word is a lamp to my feet and a light to my path. It makes my way plain before me. I do not stumble, for my steps are ordered in the Word.

The Holy Spirit leads and guides me into all the truth. He gives me understanding, discernment, and comprehension so that I am preserved from the snares of the evil one.

I delight myself in You and Your Word. Because of that, You put Your desires within my heart. I commit my way unto You, and You bring it to pass. I am confident that You are at work in me now both to will and to do all Your good pleasure.

I exalt Your Word, hold it in high esteem, and give it first place. *I make my schedule around Your Word.* I make the Word the final authority to settle all questions that confront me. I choose to agree with the Word of God, and I choose to disagree with any thoughts, conditions, or circumstances contrary to Your Word. I boldly and confidently say that my heart is fixed and established on the solid foundation—the living Word—of God! Amen.

Scripture References

Hebrews 4:12	1 Peter 3:12
Colossians 3:16	Colossians 4:2
Joshua 1:8	Ephesians 6:10
1 Peter 1:23	Luke 18:1
Psalm 91:4	James 5:16
Psalm 119:105	Psalm 37:4,5
Psalm 37:23	Philippians 2:13
Colossians 1:9	2 Corinthians 10:5
John 16:13	Psalm 112:7,8

To Watch What You Say

Father, today I make a commitment to You in the name of Jesus. I turn from speaking idle words and foolishly talking things that are contrary to my true desire. Your Word says that the tongue defiles, that the tongue sets on fire the course of nature, that the tongue is set on fire of hell.

In the name of Jesus, I submit to godly wisdom that I might learn to control my tongue. I am determined that hell will not set my tongue on fire. I renounce, reject, and repent of every word that has ever proceeded out of my mouth against You, God, and Your operation. I cancel its power and dedicate my mouth to speak excellent and right things. My mouth shall utter truth.

Because I am the righteousness of God in Christ Jesus, I set the course of my life for obedience, for abundance, for wisdom, for health, and for joy. Set a guard over my mouth, O Lord; keep watch over the door of my lips. Then the words of my mouth and my deeds shall show forth Your righteousness and Your salvation all of my days. I purpose to guard my mouth and my tongue that I might keep myself from calamity.

Father, Your words are top priority to me. They are spirit and life. I let the Word dwell in me richly in all wisdom. The ability of God is released within me by the words of my mouth and by the Word of God. I speak Your words out of my mouth. They are alive in me. You are alive and working in me. So I can boldly say that my words are words of faith, words of power, words of love, and words of life. They produce good things in my life and in the lives of others because I choose Your words for my lips, and Your will for my life, in Jesus' name. Amen.

Scripture References

Ephesians 5:4	Proverbs 21:23
2 Timothy 2:16	Ephesians 4:27
James 3:6	James 1:6
Proverbs 8:6,7	John 6:63
2 Corinthians 5:21	Colossians 3:16
Proverbs 4:23	Philemon 6

To Live Free From Worry

Father, I thank You that I have been delivered from the power of darkness and translated into the kingdom of Your dear Son. I commit to live free from worry, in the name of Jesus, for the law of the Spirit of life in Christ Jesus has made me free from the law of sin and death.

I humble myself under Your mighty hand that in due time You may exalt me. I cast the whole of my cares for myself, my spouse, my children, and my grandchildren—all my anxieties, all my worries, all my concerns—once and for all on You. You care for me affectionately and care about me watchfully. You sustain me. You will never allow the consistently righteous to be moved—made to slip, fall, or fail!

Father, I delight myself in You, and You perfect that which concerns me.

I cast down imaginations (reasonings) and every high thing that exalts itself against the knowledge of You, and I bring into captivity every thought to the obedience of Christ. I lay aside every weight and the sin of worry, which does try so easily to beset me. I run with patience the race that is set before me, looking unto Jesus, the author and finisher of my faith.

In the name of Jesus, I commit myself, my spouse, my children, and my grandchildren into Your care because I know that You are able to keep that which I have committed unto You against that day. I think on (fix my mind on) those things that are true, honest, just, pure, lovely, of good report, virtuous, and deserving of praise. I will not let my heart be troubled. I abide in Your promises concerning my children and my children's children, and Your Word abides in me. Therefore, Father, I do not forget what manner of person I am. I look into the perfect law of liberty and continue therein, being not a forgetful hearer but a doer of the Word and, thus, I am blessed in my doing!

Thank You, Father. I am carefree. I walk in that peace that passes all understanding, in Jesus' name! Amen.

Scripture References

Colossians 1:13	Hebrews 12:1,2
Romans 8:2	2 Timothy 1:12
1 Peter 5:6,7 AMP	Philippians 4:8
Psalm 55:22	John 14:1
Psalm 138:8	James 1:22-25
2 Corinthians 10:5	Philippians 4:6

Submitting All to God

Dear Grandparent:

When rebellion is overtly demonstrated in the life of a family member, it is often perceived to be an individual problem, but in reality it is a family problem. Rebellion is rooted in past generations, but the good news is that you can prepare the way for your grandchildren to decide to submit to the God who loves and cares for them, and to fulfill their destiny. The weapons of your warfare are not carnal, but mighty through God to the overthrow and tearing down of hidden family idols. Rather than focusing on the symptoms of rebellion, focus on God, the supreme authority.

Prayer

Father, I acknowledge You as the supreme authority—the God of order. It is my prayer that I will walk in submission to You, living a joyful life of victory before my grandchildren. May they understand that it is You who instituted the authority structures that support healthy relationships and maintain harmony.

Forgive us for practicing witchcraft (rebellion) and worshiping idols (stubbornness). In the name of Jesus, I loose the effects of witchcraft from my family and tear down all idols that have hindered this generation from hearing and embracing truth.

I forgive the sins of my grandchildren and bind their hearts and minds to Your goodness, which leads them to repentance. I loose thoughts of rebellion from their hearts and minds. Holy Spirit, thank You for convicting and convincing them of sin, righteousness, and judgment. Father, I ask you to bind up and heal all their emotional wounds, fill to the full their every need that they may resolve life issues.

Father, You deserve honesty from the heart; yes, utter sincerity and truthfulness. Oh, give us this wisdom. Sprinkle us with the cleansing blood, and we shall be clean again. Wash us, and we shall be whiter than snow. You have rescued us from the dominion of darkness and brought us into the kingdom of the Son You love, in whom we have redemption, the forgiveness of sins.

In the name of Jesus, I will not fear when it seems that the lives of my grandchildren are spiraling out of control. I bind my mind to the mind of Christ, my emotions to the control of the Holy Spirit. May Your will be done in their lives, even as it is in heaven.

Father, I desire to leave a legacy of faith in God, an example of a life totally surrendered to Your will for Your purposes. Then my grandchildren will know the good things You have prepared for them.

Lord, help them walk through the process of surrendering their all to You. I decree that they shall exchange rebellion and stubbornness for a willing and obedient heart. When they refuse to listen, anoint their ears to hear; when they are blinded by their own desires, open their eyes to see.

My family and future generations belong to Jesus Christ, the Anointed One, who breaks down and destroys every yoke of bondage. As each one grows in the grace and knowledge of Jesus Christ they will surrender all; will be overcomers by the blood of the Lamb and by the word of their testimony!

Surrendered to Your will, my grandchildren will have protection and dwell in the secret place of the Most High.

In Jesus' name I pray. Amen.

Scripture References

1 Corinthians 14:33   Psalm 51:6,7 TLB

1 Timothy 2:2   Colossians 1:13,14 NIV

Psalm 91:1   Matthew 10:38,39 AMP

1 Peter 5:5 AMP   John 16:33

Matthew 6:10   John 15:15

James 4:7   Revelation 12:11

1 Samuel 15:22,23 TLB

Strength To Overcome Cares and Burdens

I love You fervently *and* devotedly, O Lord, my Strength. You are my Rock, my Fortress, and my Deliverer; my God, my keen and firm Strength in whom I will trust *and* take refuge, my Shield, and the Horn of my salvation, my High Tower. I lay my burden and cares for my grandchildren at the cross, Lord, [releasing the weight of it] and You will sustain me; I thank You that You will never allow me, the [consistently] righteous, to be moved—made to slip, fall, or fail.

In the name of Jesus, I withstand the devil's tactics. I am firm in my faith [against his onset]—rooted, established, strong, immovable, and determined. Father, I thank You that Your presence goes with me and that You give me rest. I wait for You and patiently stay myself upon You. I will not fret myself, nor shall I let my heart be troubled, neither shall I let it be afraid for my grandchildren. I hope in You, God, and wait expectantly for You; for I shall yet praise You, for You are the help of my countenance and my God.

In Jesus' name I pray. Amen.

Scripture References

Psalm 42:11

James 4:6,7

Psalm 127:1

Matthew 11:28-30

Psalm 55:22

1 Peter 5:9

Hebrews 4:10,11

Exodus 33:14

Psalm 37:7

John 14:27

Psalm 42:11

Victory Over Fear

Father, when I am afraid for my grandchildren, I will put my confidence in You. Yes, I will trust Your promises to contend with those who contend with me. You will keep them safe. And since I trust You, what can mere man do to them?

You have not given me a spirit of timidity, but of power and love and discipline (sound judgment). Therefore, I am not ashamed of the testimony of my Lord. I have not received a spirit of slavery leading to fear again, but I have received a spirit of adoption as a son, by which I cry out, "Abba! Father!"

Jesus, You delivered me, who, through fear of death, had been living all my life as a slave to constant dread. I receive the gift You left me—peace of mind and heart! And the peace You give isn't fragile like the peace the world gives. I cast away troubled thoughts, and I choose not to be afraid for my grandchildren. I believe in God; I believe also in You.

Lord, You are my light and my salvation; You are my grandchildren's protection from danger—whom shall I fear? When evil men come to destroy my grandchildren, they will stumble and fall! Yes, though a mighty army marches against them, my heart shall know no fear! I am confident that You will save them for Your glory and honor.

Thank You, Holy Spirit, for bringing these things to my remembrance when I am tempted to be afraid. I will trust in my God. In the name of Jesus I pray. Amen.

Scripture References

Psalm 56:3-5 TLB

2 Timothy 1:7,8 NAS

Romans 8:15 NAS

Hebrews 2:15 TLB

John 14:1,17 TLB

Psalm 27:1-3 TLB

Health and Healing

Father, in the name of Jesus, I come before You asking You to heal me. It is written that the prayer of faith will save the sick, and the Lord will raise me up. And if I have committed sins, I will be forgiven. I let go of all unforgiveness, resentment, anger, and bad feelings toward anyone.

My body is the temple of the Holy Spirit, and I desire to be in good health. I seek truth that will make me free—both spiritual and natural (*good eating habits, medications if necessary, and appropriate rest and exercise*). You bought me at a price, and I desire to glorify You in my spirit and my body—they both belong to You.

Thank You, Father, for sending Your Word to heal me and deliver me from all my destructions. Jesus, You are the Word who became flesh and dwelt among us. You bore my griefs (pains) and carried my sorrows (sickness). You were pierced through for my transgressions and crushed for my iniquities, the chastening for my wellbeing fell upon You, and by Your scourging I am healed.

Father, I give attention to Your words and incline my ear to Your sayings. I will not let them depart from my sight, but I will keep them in the midst of my heart, for they are life and health to my whole body.

Since the Spirit of Him who raised Jesus from the dead dwells in me, He who raised Christ from the dead will also give life to my mortal body through His Spirit, who dwells in me.

Thank You that I will prosper and be in health, even as my soul prospers. Amen.

Scripture References

James 5:15 NKJV	Proverbs 4:21,22 NAS
1 Corinthians 6:19,20	Psalm 103:3-5 NAS
Psalm 107:20	Romans 8:11 NKJV
John 1:14	3 John 2
Isaiah 53:4,5 NAS	

Psalms. 103: 3-5
He forgives all my sins, and heals all my diseases - He ransoms me from death and surrounds me with love and tender mercies He fills my life with good things- My youth is renewed like the eagles!

Victory in a Healthy Lifestyle

Dear Grandparent:

Do all that you know to do to maintain a healthy lifestyle. My children enjoyed their Grandmother Griffin, who believed in exercising and eating right; she rejoiced in the Lord with dancing every day. She played with her grandchildren, laughed with them, shared their favorite snacks, and jumped on the bed with them (even though she never allowed her children to do this). She was always interested in them and what they were doing. When she went home to be with the Lord, she was pronounced by her doctor "a very young eighty-one-year-old." She enjoyed her grandchildren and left them a legacy of joy and faith.

Prayer

Father, I am Your child, and Jesus is Lord over my spirit, soul, and body. I praise You because I am fearfully and wonderfully made. Your works are wonderful; I know that full well.

Lord, thank You for declaring Your plans for me— plans to prosper me and not to harm me, plans to give me hope and a future. I choose to renew my mind to Your plans for a healthy lifestyle. You have abounded toward me in all prudence and wisdom. Therefore, I give thought to my steps. Teach me knowledge and good judgment.

My body is for You, Lord. So here is what I want to do with Your help, Father. I choose to take my everyday, ordinary life—my sleeping, eating, going-to-work, and walking-around life—and place it before You as an offering. Embracing what You do for me is the best thing I can do for You.

Christ (the Messiah) will be magnified and receive glory and praise in this body of mine and will be boldly exalted in my person. Thank You, Father, in Jesus' name! Hallelujah! Amen.

Scripture References

Psalm 139:14 NIV

Romans 12:2 NIV

Jeremiah 29:11 NIV

Proverbs 14:15 NIV

Psalm 119:66 NIV

Romans 12:1 MESSAGE

Philippians 1:20 AMP

Pleading the Blood of Jesus

I.

Morning Prayer*

Father, I come in the name of Jesus to plead His blood on my life, my children and their children, all that belongs to me, and over all which You have made me a steward.

I plead the blood of Jesus on the portals of my mind, my body (the temple of the Holy Spirit), my emotions, and my will. I believe that I am protected by the blood of the Lamb, which gives me access to the Holy of Holies.

I plead the blood on my children, on my grandchildren and their children, and on all those whom You have given me in this life.

Lord, You have said that the life of the flesh is in the blood. Thank You for this blood that has cleansed me from sin and sealed the new covenant, of which I am a partaker. In the name of Jesus I bind my children and grandchildren to the cross, to the blood of Jesus, and to the truth that makes them free.

In Jesus' name I pray. Amen.

Scripture References

Exodus 12:7,13	Leviticus 17:11
1 Corinthians 6:19	1 John 1:7
Hebrews 9:6-14	Hebrews 13:20 AMP

---

* Based on a prayer written by Joyce Meyer in *The Word, the Name and the Blood* (Tulsa: Harrison House, 1995).

II.

*Evening Prayer**

Father, as I lie down to sleep, I plead the blood of Jesus upon my life—within me, around me, and between me and all evil and the author of evil.

In Jesus' name I pray. Amen.

---

* Based on a prayer written by Mrs. C. Nuzum as recorded by Billye Brim in *The Blood and the Glory* (Tulsa: Harrison House, 1995).

Receiving a Discerning Heart

Father, I thank You for creating within me a wise and discerning heart, so that I am able to distinguish between right and wrong when I am talking with my grandchildren. I bind my emotions to the control of the Holy Spirit when they are insisting on their own way.

This is my prayer: that my love for my grandchildren may abound more and more in knowledge and depth of insight, so that I may be able to discern what is best in every situation. I desire to be pure and blameless until the day of Christ, filled with the fruit of righteousness that comes through Jesus Christ—to Your glory and praise, O Lord.

Father, I trust in You with all of my heart and lean not on my own understanding; in all of my relationships with my grandchildren I acknowledge You, and You will make my paths straight before me. Through Your precepts I get understanding; therefore, I hate every false way. Your Word is a lamp to my feet and a light to my path.

Joseph was described as a discerning and wise man who was put in charge of the entire land of Egypt. As You were with Joseph, so shall You be with me. You will cause me to find favor with my grandchildren when we are riding, walking, or sitting down for a meal.

I make [special] request, [asking] that I may be filled with the full (deep and clear) knowledge of Your will in all spiritual wisdom and in understanding and discernment of spiritual things—that I may walk (live and conduct myself before these grandchildren) in a manner worthy of You, Lord, fully pleasing to You and desiring to please You in all things, steadily growing and increasing in and by Your knowledge [with fuller, deeper, and clearer insight, acquaintance, and recognition].

Because Jesus has been made unto me wisdom, I listen and add to my learning; I discern and get guidance, understanding Your will for my grandchildren.

In the name of Jesus I pray. Amen.

Scripture References

1 Kings 3:9 NIV	Proverbs 3:1-4
Philippians 1:9-11 NIV	Colossians 1:9,10 AMP
Proverbs 3:5 NIV	1 Corinthians 1:30
Psalm 119:104,105 AMP	Proverbs 1:5
Genesis 41:39-41 NIV	Ephesians 5:17
Joshua 1:5	

Protection for Travel

Father, today, in Jesus' name, I confess Your Word over my travel plans and know that Your Word does not go out and return to You void, but it accomplishes what You say it will do. I give You thanks for moving quickly to perform Your Word and fulfill its promises.

As I prepare to travel, I rejoice in the promises that Your Word holds for the protection and safety of the righteous. Only You, Father, make me live in safety. I trust in You and dwell in Your protection. If I face any problems or trouble, I will run to You, Father, my strong tower and shelter in time of need. Believing in the written Word of God, I speak peace, safety, and success over my travel plans, in Jesus' name.

As a child of God, my path of travel is preserved, and angels keep charge over me and surround my car/airplane/train/ship. I will proceed with my travel plans without fear of accidents, problems, or any type of frustrations. I have the peace of God and will allow fear no place as I travel; the Lord delivers me from every type of evil and preserves me for His kingdom. I stand confident that my travel plans will not be disrupted or confused.

Thank You, Father, that in every situation You are there to protect me. No matter in what means of transportation I choose to travel, You have redeemed me and will protect me. The earth and all things on it are under Your command. You are my heavenly Father. Through my faith in You, I have the power to tread on serpents and have all power over the enemy. No food or water will harm me when I arrive at my destination. My travel is safe.

Father, I give You the glory in this situation. Thank You that as I keep Your ways before me, I will be safe. Your mercy is upon me and my family, and our travels will be safe. Not a hair on our heads shall perish. Thank You, Father, for Your guidance and safety. You are worthy of all praise! Amen.

Scripture References

Isaiah 55:11

Jeremiah 1:12

Psalm 4:8

Psalm 91:1

Proverbs 18:10

Proverbs 29:25

Mark 11:23,24

Proverbs 2:8

Psalm 91:11,12

2 Timothy 4:18

Philippians 4:7

2 Timothy 1:7

Isaiah 43:1-3

2 Timothy 4:18

Hosea 2:18

Luke 10:19

Psalm 91:13

Luke 21:18

Mark 16:18

Matthew 18:18

John 14:13

Daniel 9:18

Luke 1:50

Abiding in Jesus

Dear Grandparent:

> **Let no one say when he is tempted, I am tempted from God; for God is incapable of being tempted by [what is] evil and He Himself tempts no one. But every person is tempted when he is drawn away, enticed and baited by his own evil desire (lust, passions). Then the evil desire, when it has conceived, gives birth to sin, and sin, when it is fully matured, brings forth death.**
>
> **James 1:13-15 AMP**

Single people sometimes express the difficulty of keeping themselves pure. Some have asked, "Doesn't God understand that we are only human? Why did He create us with desires? Surely He understands and excuses us when we fall into temptation. If He wants me to avoid sexual temptation, then why doesn't He send me the spouse I have asked Him to give me?"

The Scriptures condemn premarital sex, fornication, adultery, and all forms of sexual perversion. (Matt. 15:19; Mark 7:21 AMP; Gal. 5:19-21; Col. 3:5,6.) Although sexual desires are not a sin, if not properly controlled, they can lead to sin.

According to James 1:13-15, sin begins with a thought conceived from lust. Lust is not limited to sex. It is possible to lust after many things that can cause sin. That's why it is so important to take control over the mind and heart to keep them pure and holy in spite of temptation.

One snare for many single people is the mistaken idea that marriage will automatically release them from the temptation to sin. Without repentance and the renewing of the mind, those who have a problem with lustful thoughts before they are married will have the same problem after they are married, just as those who have a problem with sexual perversion before marriage will continue to have the same problem after marriage.

One married man shared his testimony of deliverance from pornography. He was having to continually guard himself from mental images that kept reappearing. Marriage is not a cure-all for sexual sins or any other sin.

Yes, God does understand. With every temptation He has provided a way of escape. (1 Cor. 10:13.) Yes, there is forgiveness for sin through God's abounding grace. (1 John 1:9; Rom. 5:20.) The question is, "...Are we to remain in sin in order that God's grace (favor and mercy) may multiply and overflow? Certainly not! How can we who died to sin live in it any longer?" (Rom. 6:1,2 AMP).

We who are in Christ desire to bring glory to the Father. We cannot do so in our own strength. It is abiding in union with Jesus and loving as Jesus loves that ensures answered prayers. (John 15:7-9.) If our prayers are not being answered, it is time to check our love walk. We must ask ourselves, "Are we keeping ourselves in the love of God—remaining vitally united with Jesus?"

We know [absolutely] that anyone born of God does not [deliberately and knowingly] practice committing sin, but the One who was begotten of God carefully watches over and protects him [Christ's divine presence within him preserves him against the evil], and the wicked one does not lay hold (get a grip) on him or touch [him].

1 John 5:18 AMP

This verse says that the wicked one cannot touch us. What is the condition? Having Christ's presence within, staying united with Him—abiding in Him and allowing His Word to abide in us.

If you want to abide in Christ and have His Word abide in you, pray the following prayer with a sincere and believing heart.

Prayer

Lord, I am abiding in Your Word [holding fast to Your teachings and living in accordance with them]. It is my desire to be Your true disciple. I am abiding in (vitally united to) the vine. I cannot bear fruit unless I abide in You.

Lord, because You are the vine and I am a branch living in You, I bear much (abundant) fruit. Apart from You [cut off from vital union with You], I can do nothing. Your Son, Jesus, said, "If you live in Me [abide vitally united to Me] and My words remain in you and continue to live in your hearts, ask whatever you will, and it shall be done for you" (John 15:7 AMP).

When I bear (produce) much fruit, You, Father, are honored and glorified. By Your grace that I have received, I will show and prove myself to be a true follower of Your Son, Jesus. He has loved me, [just] as You, Father, have loved Him. I am abiding in that love.

Lord, You have assured me that if I keep Your commandments [if I continue to obey Your instructions], I will abide in Your love and live in it, just as Your Son, Jesus, obeyed Your commandments and lived in Your love. He told me these things that Your joy and delight may be in me and that my joy and gladness may be of full measure and complete and overflowing. This is Your commandment: that we love one another [just] as You have loved us.

Father, thank You for Your Word—it is the truth that makes me free. I am born (begotten) of You, Lord, and I do not [deliberately, knowingly, and habitually] practice sin. Your nature abides in me [Your principle of life remains permanently within me]; and I cannot practice sinning because I am born (begotten) of You. I have hidden Your Word in my heart that I might not sin against You.

May Christ through my faith [actually] dwell (settle down, abide, make His permanent home) in my heart! It is my desire to be rooted deep in love and founded securely on love, that I may have the power and be strong to apprehend and grasp with all the saints [Your devoted people, the experience of that love] what is the breadth and length and height and depth [of it].

I pray, in the name of Jesus, that I may know this love that surpasses knowledge—that I may be filled to the measure of all Your fullness. Now to You who are able to do immeasurably more than all I ask or imagine, according to Your power that is at work within me, to You be glory in the church and in Christ Jesus throughout all generations, forever and ever! Amen.

Scripture References

John 8:31 AMP	1 John 3:9 AMP
John 15:4,5 AMP	Psalm 119:11
John 15:7-12 AMP	Ephesians 3:17,18 AMP
John 8:32	Ephesians 3:19-21 NIV
John 17:17	

Letting Go of Bitterness

Dear Grandparent:

In interviews with divorced men and women, I have been encouraged to write a prayer on overcoming bitterness. Often the injustice of the situation in which these people find themselves creates deep hurts, wounds in the spirit, and anger that is so near the surface that the individuals involved risk sinking into the trap of bitterness and revenge. Their thoughts may turn inward as they consider the unfairness of the situation and dwell on how badly they have been treated.

In a family divorce situation, bitterness sometimes distorts ideas of what is best for the child/children involved. One parent (and sometimes both parents) will use the child/children against the other. Unresolved anger often moves one marriage partner to hurt the one he or she holds responsible for his or her pain and sense of betrayal.

There is healing available. There is a way of escape for all who will turn to the Healer, obeying Him and trusting Him. Grandparent, if your child and grandchildren have experienced the pain of divorce, you can be an instrument of healing. Guard against taking up the offense toward those who have wronged your family, and keep your heart pure. Your grandchildren need your love and your expression of forgiveness toward those who have mistreated them.

Prayer

Father, life is so unfair at times. The pain of rejection is almost more than my children and grandchildren can bear. Father, You see the strife, anger, rejection, and separation they are experiencing. I come before You to stand in the gap for them, repair the walls, and build up the hedge of protection round about them.

Lord, help my son/daughter and grandchildren let go of all bitterness and indignation and wrath (passion, rage, bad temper) and resentment (anger, animosity).

You are the One who binds up and heals the brokenhearted. In the name of Jesus I release Your anointing that destroys every yoke of bondage, and believe that they will receive emotional healing. It is You who will give them the grace to stand firm until the process is complete.

Thank You for wise counselors. I acknowledge You, Holy Spirit, as their wonderful Counselor. Thank You for helping my son/daughter and grandchildren as they work out their salvation with fear and trembling, for it is You, Father, who works in them to will and to act according to Your good purpose.

In the name of Jesus, I bind them to Your grace and forgiveness and believe that they will choose to forgive those who have wronged them. Help them live a life of forgiveness because You have forgiven them. I loose all bad feelings toward others—bitterness, rage, anger, brawling, and slander, along with every form of malice—from their hearts, minds, and attitudes.

With Your help, Holy Spirit, I make every effort to be a good example to my family members, living in peace with all people. I will be holy, for I know that without holiness no one will see You, Lord. I purpose to see to it that I do not miss Your grace and that no bitter root grows up within me to cause trouble.

I will watch and pray, that I enter not into temptation or cause others to stumble.

Thank You, Father, that You watch over Your Word to perform it and that the one whom the Son has set free is free indeed. I declare that I have overcome resentment and bitterness by the blood of the Lamb and by the word of my testimony, and my children and grandchildren will know that they can too.

In Jesus' name I pray. Amen.

Scripture References

Ephesians 4:31 AMP

Luke 4:18

Isaiah 10:27

Proverbs 11:14

John 15:26 AMP

Philippians 2:12,13 NIV

Matthew 5:44

Ephesians 4:31,32 NIV

Hebrews 12:14,15 NIV

Matthew 26:41

Romans 14:21

Jeremiah 1:12 AMP

John 8:36

Revelation 12:11

Developing Patience

Father, I come before You in the name of Jesus. I
desire to meditate, consider, and inquire in Your presence.
I am asking for Your help in developing patience, quietly
entrusting my future to Your will.

By Your grace I surrender my life—all my desires, all
that I am, and all that I am not—to the control of the
Holy Spirit, who produces this kind of fruit in me: love,
joy, peace, patience, kindness, goodness, faithfulness,
gentleness, and self-control; and here there is no conflict. I
belong to Jesus Christ, and I seek to live by the Holy
Spirit's power and to follow the Holy Spirit's leading in
every part of my life. [In exercising] self-control I
[develop] steadfastness (patience, endurance), and in
[exercising] steadfastness I [develop] godliness (piety).

By faith, I consider it wholly joyful whenever I am
enveloped in, or encounter, trials of any sort or fall into
various temptations. It is then that I am reminded to rest
assured and understand that the trial and proving of my
faith brings out endurance and steadfastness and
patience. I purpose to let endurance and steadfastness and
patience have full play and do a thorough work, so that I
may be perfectly and fully developed [with no defects],
lacking in nothing.

Father, fill me with the knowledge of Your will through all spiritual wisdom and understanding. Then I will live a life worthy of You and will please You in every way: bearing fruit in every good work. I ask You to help me grow in the knowledge of You, so that I might be strengthened with all power according to Your glorious might. Then I know that I will have great endurance and patience, and I will joyfully give thanks to You. I thank You for qualifying me to share in the inheritance of the saints in the kingdom of light.

Father, I strip off and throw aside every encumbrance (unnecessary weight) and that sin which so readily (deftly and cleverly) clings to and entangles me, and I run with patient endurance and steady and active persistence the appointed course of the race that is set before me. I look away [from all that will distract] to Jesus, who is the leader and the source of my faith [giving the first incentive for my belief] and is also its finisher [bringing it to maturity and perfection].

With patience I am able to persevere through the difficult times—times of anxiety and worry—and overcome fear. I am an overcomer by the blood of the Lamb and by the word of my testimony.

In Jesus' name I pray. Amen.

Scripture References

Psalm 27:4,8 AMP

Psalm 3:4 AMP

Psalm 37:4,5

Galatians 5:22-25 TLB

2 Peter 1:6 AMP

James 1:2-4 AMP

Colossians 1:9-12 NIV

Hebrews 12:1,2 AMP

Revelation 12:11

Protection From Terrorism

Father, in the name of Jesus, I praise You and offer up thanksgiving because the Lord is near—He is coming soon. Therefore, I will not fret or have any anxiety about the safety of my children and grandchildren, whether they are near or far. Terrorism is all around, but we will not fear man. If God be for us, who can be against us?

Jesus, You have given us the authority and power to trample upon serpents and scorpions and (physical and mental strength and ability) over all the power that the enemy [possesses], and nothing shall in any way harm us. You are seated at the right hand of the Father far above principality, power, might, and dominion (including terrorism) not only in this age but also in that which is to come, and I am seated together with Him.

In the name of Jesus, I take authority over a spirit of timidity—of cowardice, of craven and cringing and fawning fear (of terrorism)—for [God has given me a spirit] of power and of love and of a calm and well-balanced mind and discipline and self-control.

My family and I shall not be afraid of the terror of the night, nor of the arrow [the evil plots and slanders of the wicked] that flies by day, nor of the pestilence that stalks in darkness, nor of the destruction and sudden death that surprise and lay waste at noonday.

Therefore, we are established on righteousness, rightness—[right], in conformity with God's will and order; we shall be far from even the thought of oppression or destruction, for we shall not fear, and from terror, for it shall not come near us.

Holy Spirit, thank You for writing this Word upon the tablets of our hearts so that we can speak it out of our mouths with confidence, for we will order our conversation aright, and You will show us the salvation of God. Hallelujah! Amen.

Scripture References

Philippians 4:5,6 AMP	Psalm 56:9 AMP
2 Timothy 1:7 AMP	Luke 10:19 AMP
Ephesians 1:20-23	Psalm 91:5,6 AMP
Ephesians 2:6	Isaiah 54:14 AMP
Proverbs 3:3 AMP	Psalm 50:23
Matthew 16:19	

*To Receive Jesus as Your Lord and Savior**

Father, it is written in Your Word that if I confess with my mouth that Jesus is Lord and believe in my heart that You have raised Him from the dead, I shall be saved. Therefore, Father, I confess that Jesus is my Lord. I make Him Lord of my life right now. I believe in my heart that You raised Jesus from the dead. I renounce my past life with Satan and close the door to any of his devices.

I thank You for forgiving me of all my sin. Jesus is my Lord, and I am a new creation. Old things have passed away; now all things become new in Jesus' name. Amen.

Scripture References

Romans 10:9,10	John 16:8,9
1 John 1:9	Romans 5:8
2 Corinthians 5:17	John 14:6
John 3:16	Romans 10:13
John 6:37	Ephesians 2:1-10
John 10:10	John 1:12
Romans 3:23	2 Corinthians 5:21
2 Corinthians 5:19	

* If you prayed this prayer to receive Jesus Christ as your Savior for the first time, please contact us on the Web at www.harrisonhouse.com or write to us at Harrison House, P.O. Box 35035, Tulsa, Oklahoma 74153 to receive a free book.

To Be Filled With the Spirit

My heavenly Father, I am Your child, for I believe in my heart that Jesus has been raised from the dead, and I have confessed Him as my Lord.

Jesus said, "How much more will your heavenly Father give the Holy Spirit to those who ask Him!" (Luke 11:13 NKJV). I ask You now in the name of Jesus to fill me with the Holy Spirit. I step into the fullness and power that I desire in the name of Jesus. I confess that I am a Spirit-filled Christian. As I yield my vocal organs, I expect to speak in tongues, for the Spirit gives me utterance in the name of Jesus. Praise the Lord! Amen.

Scripture References

Romans 10:9,10	Acts 10:44-46
John 14:16,17	Acts 19:2,5,6
Luke 11:13	Romans 10:9,10
Acts 1:8	1 Corinthians 14:2-15
Acts 2:4	1 Corinthians 14:18,27
Acts 2:32,33,39	Ephesians 6:18
Acts 8:12-17	Jude 1:20

About the Author

Germaine Griffin Copeland, founder and president of Word Ministries, Inc., is the bestselling author of the *Prayers That Avail Much®* family of books. Her writings provide scriptural prayer instruction to help you pray effectively for those things that concern you and your family and for other prayer assignments.

Germaine is the daughter of the late Reverend A. H. "Buck" and Donnis Brock Griffin. She and her husband, Everette, have four children and eleven grandchildren. Their prayer assignments increase as great-grandchildren are born into the family. Germaine and Everette reside in Roswell, a suburb of Atlanta, Georgia.

MISSION STATEMENT
WORD MINISTRIES, INC.

Motivating individuals to pray,
Encouraging them to achieve intimacy with God,
Bringing emotional wholeness and spiritual growth

You may contact Word Ministries by writing:

Word Ministries, Inc.
38 Sloan Street
Roswell, Georgia 30075
or calling 770-518-1065

www.prayers.org

*Please include your testimonies
and praise reports when you write.*

Other Books by Germaine Copeland

Prayers That Avail Much 25th Anniversary Commemorative Gift Edition

Prayers That Avail Much 25the Anniversary Commemorative Leather Edition

Prayers That Avail Much for the Workplace

Prayers That Avail Much Volume 1

Prayers That Avail Much Volume 2

Prayers That Avail Much Volume 3

Prayers That Avail Much for Singles

Prayers That Avail Much for Men—hardbound

Prayers That Avail Much for Men—pocket edition

Prayers That Avail Much for Women—hardbound

Prayers That Avail Much for Women—pocket edition

Prayers That Avail Much for Mothers—hardbound

Prayers That Avail Much for Moms—pocket edition

Prayers That Avail Much for Teens—hardbound

Prayers That Avail Much for Teens—mass market

Prayers That Avail Much for the College Years

Prayers That Avail Much for Graduates

Oraciones Con Poder—*Prayers That Avail Much* (Spanish Edition)

Available at fine bookstores everywhere or from www.harrisonhouse.com.

MORE PRAYERS THAT AVAIL MUCH!

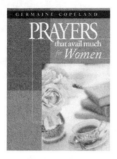 If this book has been a blessing to you, these dynamic prayers are available in their entirety in the clothbound edition of *Prayers That Avail Much*®. Check with your local bookstore or visit us at www.harrisonhouse.com.

Prayers That Avail Much for Women
ISBN 1-57794-489-5

*Prayers That Avail Much
for Mothers*
ISBN 1-57794-490-9

*Prayers That Avail Much
for Men*
ISBN 1-57794-182-9

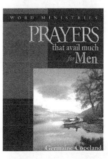

*Prayers That Avail Much
for Teens*
ISBN 1-57794-491-7

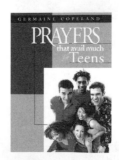

www.harrisonhouse.com

Fast. Easy. Convenient!

- ◆ New Book Information
- ◆ Look Inside the Book
- ◆ Press Releases
- ◆ Bestsellers

- ◆ Free E-News
- ◆ Author Biographies
- ◆ Upcoming Books
- ◆ Share Your Testimony

For the latest in book news and author information, please visit us on the Web at www.harrisonhouse.com. Get up-to-date pictures and details on all our powerful and life-changing products. Sign up for our e-mail newsletter, *Friends of the House,* and receive free monthly information on our authors and products including testimonials, author announcements, and more!

Harrison House—
Books That Bring Hope, Books That Bring Change

The Harrison House Vision

Proclaiming the truth and the power

Of the Gospel of Jesus Christ

With excellence;

Challenging Christians to

Live victoriously,

Grow spiritually,

Know God intimately.

Germaine Copeland has reached a generation of us who can help our grandchildren step into their destiny. How? Through persistent, power-packed prayers. As a praying grandmother myself, I truly appreciate all the ways Germaine has suggested we pray for those precious ones God has placed in our families. I'm sure you will be as excited, blessed, and encouraged as I am by this book. You'll want to refer to it every day as you pray specifically for your grandchildren.

Quin Sherrer, author
Prayers From a Grandma's Heart

Prayers That Avail Much for Grandparents is a book for me personally, as I am a grandmother myself. God is speaking about the need to connect the generations, and there is no more vital way this can be done than through prayer. Thank you, Germaine! Our children and grandchildren will rise up to thank you also!

Cindy Jacobs
Generals International

For years now, Germaine Copeland's *Prayers That Avail Much* series of books have impacted the prayer lives of countless Christians of all denominations. As pastors, these books are treasures placed in the hands of parishioners whose heart cry remains "Lord, teach us to pray."

Now as new grandparents ourselves, this new book enables us to "return the Word" regarding our newest members of the congregation. We highly recommend this book to all grandparents who desire to pray the Word over their grandchildren.

Joe & Linda Wingo, Pastors
Emmanuel Praise Church
Home of Angel Food Ministries